5 VERY GOOD REASONS
TO PUNCH A
DOLPHIN
IN THE MOUTH
(AND OTHER USEFUL GUIDES)

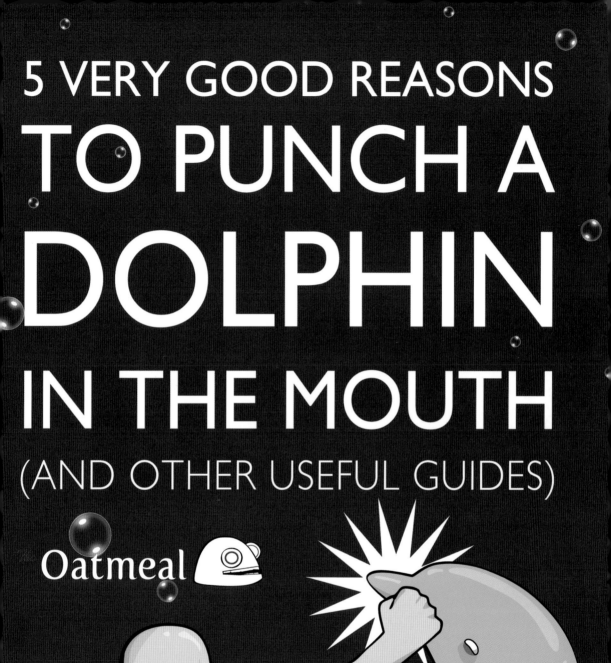

5 VERY GOOD REASONS
TO PUNCH A
DOLPHIN
IN THE MOUTH
(AND OTHER USEFUL GUIDES)

Oatmeal

Andrews McMeel
Publishing, LLC

Kansas City · Sydney · London

5 VERY GOOD REASONS TO PUNCH A DOLPHIN IN THE MOUTH

Andrews McMeel Publishing, LLC
an Andrews McMeel Universal company
1130 Walnut Street, Kansas City, Missouri 64106

www.andrewsmcmeel.com

11 12 13 14 15 TEN 10 9 8

ISBN: 978-1-4494-0116-0

Library of Congress Control Number: 2010930546

ATTENTION: SCHOOLS AND BUSINESSES
Andrews McMeel books are available at quantity discounts with bulk purchase for educational,
business, or sales promotional use. For information, please e-mail the Andrews McMeel Publishing
Special Sales Department: specialsales@amuniversal.com

INTRODUCTION

Up until the spring of 2009, I created websites for a living. I started when I was a teenager and endured fourteen years of soul-sucking meetings, hot pink logos, and clients who demanded that their corporate website play music and display animated photos of their pet. Fed up and looking for a career change, I quit my job as a designer and started drawing comics. The Oatmeal was born and subsequently made its home at http://theoatmeal.com.

After launching the website, people liked it enough that I eventually got to turn it into a book. *5 Very Good Reasons to Punch a Dolphin in the Mouth* is that book, and it contains all the comics I created in the year after I quit my job to become a comic artist. It also has an additional twenty-seven never-before-seen comics that aren't available on the web.

This book contains gorillas, prostitution, poop jokes, small quantities of chainsaws, large quantities of man nipples, and one drug-addicted dinosaur. Its purpose is to entertain, inform, and offend.

I hope you like it. If not, I hope a large meteor finds its way across the universe and smashes directly into your crotch while you sleep.

Hugs and kisses!

—The Oatmeal

8 REASONS TO KEEP A CANADIAN AS A PET

THEY'll MAKE YOU LOOK TAN

Hey, that guy looks like a big pile of mayonnaise! Let's all point and laugh.

HAHAHAHA BA HAHAHAHA HAHA HA HA HAHAHAHAHA HAHA

THEY'RE NOT PICKY EATERS

I made your favorite: Caribou brains mixed with dirty snow.

YOU'LL MEET NEW PEOPLE

FETCH! SMACK

OMG he's playing fetch with an adorable little Canadian! He must be a nice guy!

SWOON SWOON SWOON SWOON

YOU'LL ALWAYS APPEAR INNOCENT

What's going on here? What's with the shov-- Oh wait, I see you have a Canadian with you. Carry on, gentlemen.

THEY'RE HANDY IN COLD WEATHER

Man, what a snowstorm! Luckily I've got my Canadian on.

THEY'RE FUN TO HIKE WITH

MUSH! MUSH I SAY! MUSH YOU GAWDAMN CANADIAN!

THEY'RE GOOD FOR EXERCISE

THEY'RE USEFUL AROUND THE HOUSE

BRAAAAAAAAP

Why it's better 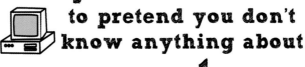 to pretend you don't know anything about computers

It happens to the best of us.

A friend or family member asks for help;

being so close, how can you say no?

Usually it begins with a small favor.

That small favor leads to others.

Once you fix something,

they'll forever regard you as the

"computer genius."

If it reaches this point, you're pretty much screwed.

From now on, they won't call tech support— they'll call *you*.

Eventually they'll rely on you for all their pirated software, games, and music.

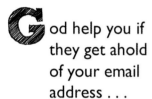

God help you if they get ahold of your email address . . .

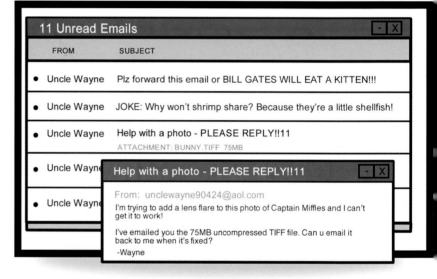

. . . **O**r your Facebook.

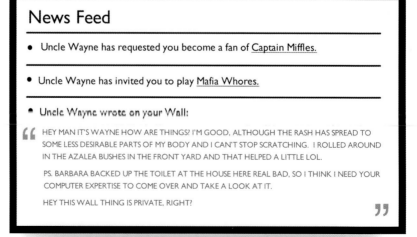

They might even ask you to make them a website.

So after the 20 minute flash intro, have the "click to enter" button appear and then burst into flames, but make it jump around so the user has to chase it

Also, my budget for this website is $10.00 But we're family, so it's cool, right?

You'll soon become technical support for all things, not just computers.

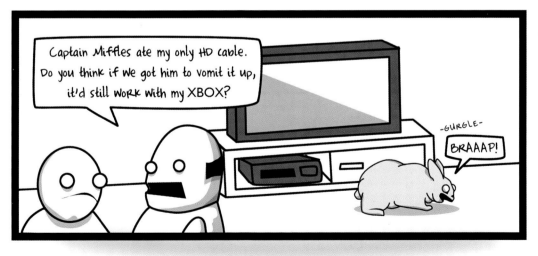

Captain Miffles ate my only HD cable. Do you think if we got him to vomit it up, it'd still work with my XBOX?

-GURGLE-

BRAAAP!

HOW TO PEE LIKE A
CHAMP

Stand
as close to one another as possible.

This makes it easier to talk about manly things.

Groan *loudly while you pee.*

This is a way of complimenting your penis for doing such a magnificent job.

If **the man next to you passes gas,** you should pass gas in return. It's like high-fiving each other with methane.

(and it would be very rude not to return a high-five)

If **there's a nice breeze,** then it's perfectly acceptable to drop your pants.

When you run out of pee,

shake your penis vigorously to remove
the excess pee. Do this for 2–5 minutes.

*The prolonged shaking reminds your little man that
although you love him, you're still in charge.*

Try to time it so that you finish

at the same time as the man next to you.

*This way you can wash your hands together
and remark on the experience.*

The 9 Types of
Crappy Handshakes

The Bone Crusher

The Politician

Those who shake with both hands
are trying to sell you something.

The Misfire

Your fingers don't quite come together like they should,
but you stick it out anyway to avoid looking awkward.

Ok something is
definitely off...

The Limp, Dead Fish

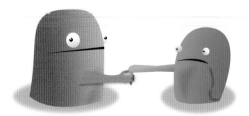

The Never-Let-Go

The Close Shaker

Really what they want is a hug.

The Hipster

Their confusing handshake makes you feel out of touch.

Sweaty McSweaterson

The Airball

Ten Words You Need To Stop Misspelling

Lose
↓
Opposite of win

Pretend the extra O is a hemorrhoid on the word. Hemorrhoids are <u>never</u> tight.

Loose
↓
Not tight

man, I've got the WORST hemorrhoid

TIGHT, BRO!

Their

Their is possessive, meaning it owns something.

I hate our new neighbors.

Their cow keeps eating the leftover casserole.

In this case, *their* is referring to the neighbors who own a cow.

They're

They're is a contraction for "they are."

They're gonna get a shovel to the face unless they get that cow under control.

No one eats my casserole.

In this case, *they're* means "they are."

There

There refers to a place or idea. Use this form if you're unsure.

Look over there!

An alien just burst out of that cow's chest!

In this case, *there* is referring to a location.

Abstract usage! I love it!

It can also refer to something more abstract:
There are many reasons to discipline a cow. For starters, a cow who eats rancid casserole will later become a host for alien parasites.

Weird

Not wierd

↓
e then i

Remember it like this:

> We ... ir ... d =
> We ... are (ir) ... dangerous (d)
> to those dumb, dirty dolphins.

Every time you spell it this way,
a dolphin gets run over by a jet ski.

Definitely

There is no A in "definitely." To help you remember, use this:

> *If you put an A in "definitely," then you're definitely an A-hole.*

Your   You're

↑   **↑**

> These both use the same rules as "their" and "they're."

Your is possessive.
In other words, you own something.

Your new baby alien loves to cuddle, but he keeps crapping in your refrigerator at night.

> This is referring to your alien
> and your refrigerator.

You're is a contraction of "you are."

You're definitely cleaning out the fridge tomorrow morning, assuming that little beast can't keep his bowels in check.

> This translates to "you are
> definitely cleaning..."

It's

⬇

This is a contraction for *it is* or *it has.*
If you can replace *it's* with *it is* or *it has*, then use *it's* in your sentence.

For example:

It's not fair that Randy gets to ride a wolverine to school, but I have to ride this stupid manatee!

Its

⬇

This is indicating possession.
Use this when one thing owns another.

For example:

The wolverine knows only death, pain, and slaughter. Also, Its thick, black fur is good for exfoliating the thighs during a long ride.

⬆

Using "it's" in this case would result in:

"Also, it is thick black fur is good for…"

which is wrong and anyone who does this deserves to be mauled by a wolverine.

Effect   Affect

Most of the time *effect* is a noun and *affect* is a verb.

If you're unsure, try substituting a different verb and see if it works.

As a child, he was affected by his parents.
As a child, he was ~~affected~~ eaten by his parents.

⬆

A verb works here so you should use "affected."

C'MERE, RANDALL
I want to ingest you, just like I did your obnoxious parakeet

You ate him?!!
But he sang only of love and beauty!
You're a monster, Dad!

Weather

⬇️

Snow, rain, sunshine, typhoons. All that crap.

I'm the sun, I make super happy sunshine! Also, one day I'll explode and burn you all alive like the miserable little sausages that you are!

Whether

⬇️

Whether is used in this way:
Your correct usage of this word will determine whether or not I kick you in the hemorrhoids.

Nothing gets a point across like a solid kick to the hemmies.

Alot

⬆️

Always leave a space here.
Remember, there's a lot of space in outer space.

Alot is not a word.

You don't write
alittle, abunch, acantaloupe, aporkchop
So don't write *alot*.

Then

is used for time.
First I stole a panda bear, then we drank malt liquor together.

The sequence of actions indicates time: first stealing the panda, and then drinking.

Than

is used for comparison.
I'm much better than a panda bear at holding my liquor.

This is comparing a panda's drinking ability with your own, so you should use "than."

HRNNNGGGGGGG BLORCH!

FAILED BEARCUT

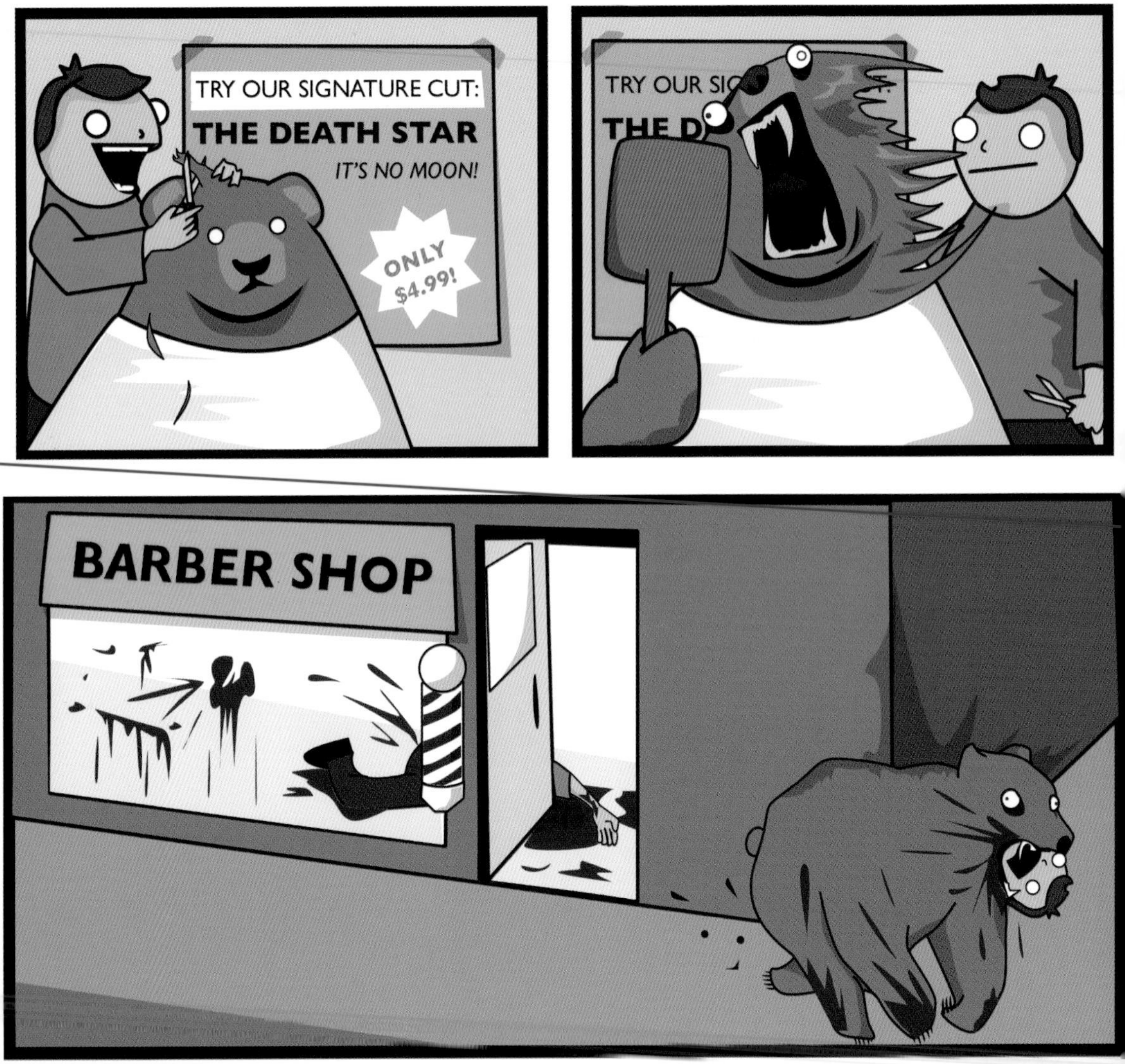
TRY OUR SIGNATURE CUT:
THE DEATH STAR
IT'S NO MOON!
ONLY $4.99!
TRY OUR SIG
THE D
BARBER SHOP

5 Very Good Reasons
to Punch a Dolphin in the Mouth

When a dolphin makes those cute whistles and clicking sounds, they're actually vulgar insults.

your mom is eeeeeeeeeasy!

Their rubbery, soft skin is easy on the knuckles and makes for a great undersea punching bag.

Dolphins play their entire lives. Humans only play until we reach adulthood—this is unfair. Make it fair by landing a roundhouse kick to the face.

Dolphins love to think that they're the strongest and the fastest. Ever seen them swim with a boat? To them it's a race. Put them in their place with a solid left hook to the jaw.

Anything that smiles that often needs to be reminded that the world is a cruel, dark place.

14 (ish) Things Worth Knowing About Cheese

SO DELICIOUS! GIVES ME CHEESERAGE

Cheese comes from milk (no surprise there)

First, that milk is heated and bacteria are added.

Bacteria in milk? This is madness!

MADNESS? THIS. IS. CHEEEEEEEESE!

These bacteria are often added in the form of yogurt or buttermilk.

Streptococcus is one type of bacteria which is commonly used. This same bacteria is what causes strep throat and meningitis.

The bacteria produce **lactic acid,** which is necessary for the milk to curdle.

After the bacteria, rennet is added.

Rennet comes from the stomach lining of mammals, where it helps digest the milk of the animal's mother.

This is supposedly how cheese was **discovered.**

Early nomadic tribes used animal organs for transport. Milk stored in these organs would have naturally mixed with rennet and bacteria. This movement would have caused the milk to  curdle and produce cheese.

Whoah! My goat intestine backpack created cheese. Best. Backpack. EVER!

The rennet

causes the milk to separate into

Whey  Curds

The whey is drained off and only the curds remain.

Go a-whey, stupid whey! GET IT?

hahaha good one!

Ooooh buRned! BetteR Rub some aloe on that buRn!

The curds are what later become cheese.
(They're like little cheese fetuses.)

We'Re being a-salt-ed! GET IT?

Shut up with the puns! We'Re being smooshed!

Next, the curds
are salted and typically
squished together.

The squished curds are
left alone for awhile

until they become

By combining ouR poweRs, we aRe now mega ultRa cuRd!

Cheese!

Some cheeses are left to age.

Others are eaten right away.

 I have a long, cheesy life ahead of me full of awe and wondeR.

I was boRn a fReak. K-K-K-KILL MEEEE

Aged:

Cheddar, swiss, parmesan, blue cheese, and gouda.

Fresh:

Mozzarella, cottage cheese, ricotta, and cream cheese.

The milk
used to make cheese can come from:

Cows   Buffalo
Horses
Camels   Goats
Human beings

Gross, huh?
There's a restaurant in NY where they actually serve cheese made from breast milk. They named the dish "Mommy's milk cheese."

Foot odor
is caused by a bacteria called *brevibacterium linens*. This same bacteria is used to create Limburger cheese, which has a strong and often unpleasant odor.

I couldn't help but notice the delicious aRoma of sweaty feet coming from youR cheese. May I have a bite?

haha no. go away.

What's in your cheese?

Blue Cheese
Penicillium cultures which produce blue-green mold.

Sharp, salty flavor. Pungent smell.

Feta Cheese
Made from sheep and goat's milk.

Tangy flavor, crumbles easily.

Cheddar
Undergoes *cheddaring*, whereby the curds are kneaded and turned.

Sharp flavor, often hard cheese.

Swiss
Full of holes caused by bacteria consuming lactic acid which releases CO_2.

The larger the holes, the stronger the flavor.

Brie
White, moldy crust with grayish cheese underneath.

Soft, flavor has a hint of ammonia.

Mozzarella
Made using spinning and cutting. *Mozzare* means "to cut."

Semi-soft, high moisture content.

Dreams are affected by cheese!

A study in 2005 by the British Cheese Board concluded that cheese had a positive effect on sleep and that eating different types of cheese before sleeping produced different dreams.

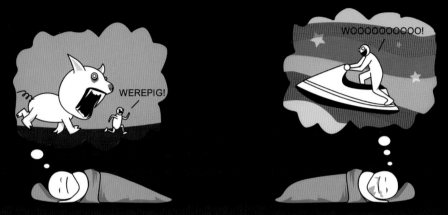

How does white milk become orange cheese?

Originally, cows would eat plants high in beta-carotene, the yellow compound found in carrots and vegetables. This resulted in cows producing yellow-orange milk.

Now, most cheesemakers just dye their cheese.

If you are **lactose intolerant** (pronounced *lactarded*) your stomach cannot process dairy.

However, cheddar and other aged cheeses contain almost none of the lactose found in milk.

How to Suck at facebook

The Gamer

The invites and updates will never stop.

— Want to join my FarmVille?!

I just upgraded my pigs to Level 13 Pork Knights! *

When they reach levels 14, 15, 16 and onto level 83 Pig Warlocks, I'll post it here!

* I've never actually played FarmVille, but any game worth playing has to have Pork Knights.

The Event Coordinator

They invite everyone to everything.

You should come to my cat's birthday party!

You've never met my cat, and you barely know me. We met for a few minutes at a party two years ago.

Since then, I've moved to Prostate, Nebrahoma. It's 2,000 miles away from you, but it'd really mean a lot if you came!

The Desperate Marketer

Their idea of marketing on Facebook is to spam all their friends with "become a fan of [whatever]" requests.
Usually [whatever] is either themselves or a paying client.

Would you like to become a fan of my website, Chads-Porkchop-Shop.com?

No? What about just becoming a fan of me instead: Chad Chumperson.

What about Photos-of-Chad.com?

Still no? How about Chads-grandma.net?

Please...fan something? Anything? Oh God please...

The Horrible Photo Tagger

They will tag ANYTHING, regardless of whether or not it's something you want your family or co-workers to see.

▸ Matt has tagged a <u>photo of you</u>

▸ Matt Writes:

"I snapped this photo last night when you barfed up nachos and peppermint schnapps into that hooker's eyes! ROFL"

The Quiz Taker

You'd think everyone had gotten sick of these by now.

▶ Christy took the quiz:

What kind of rancid meat are you?

I AM A ROTTING BUFFALO CARCASS!

▶ Christy took the quiz:

Which Backstreet Boy testicle are you?

I am Howie's left nut!

Backstreet's back ALRIGHT!

The Passive Aggressor

They post well-rehearsed retorts without mentioning anyone by name.

Oh no, you did **not** just say that to me.

I am my own **free spirit** - individual and brave.

So brave, in fact, I post updates on facebook because I'm too afraid to actually stand up to someone in person. Either that or I'm just trying to make my life look dramatic.

The Infant Profile

They use their kid as their profile picture. It's supposed to be cute, but to everyone else it's annoying and a little bit disturbing.

Bill Pickleburg

so hungover right now, need a burrito

Wall   Info   Photos

Write something ...

Married to Cindy Pickleburg

Born September 19, 1979

Interests: Beer, Porn, BBQ, female mud wrestling

Rob wrote:

dooood you were so drunk last night you kicked the bouncer right in the hemorrhoids!

Cindy wrote:

Hey sexy! Last night was pretty steamy - like one of those steamer bags full of vegetables, except it involved penises and vaginas instead of carrots.

The Rash

This person will follow you around facebook and comment on *everything* you do.

HAHAHA LOL good one!! You are the funniest dood EVAR!

You have nice eyes, has anyone ever told you that? They're like little peaches.

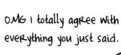

The Filterless

They'll post updates about everything, even when it's something you'd never, ever want to know.

Hey everybody, I just took a dump and it's shaped like a mountain lion!

OMG I totally agree with everything you just said.

I'll agree with anything you say, actually.

Where are you going? PAY ATTENTION TO ME, DAMNIT

C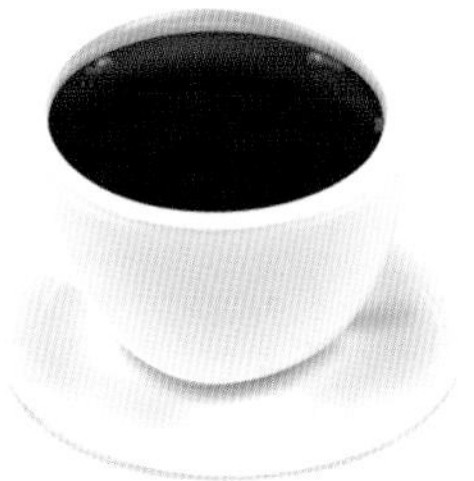FFEE

WITH & WITHOUT

WITH WITHOUT

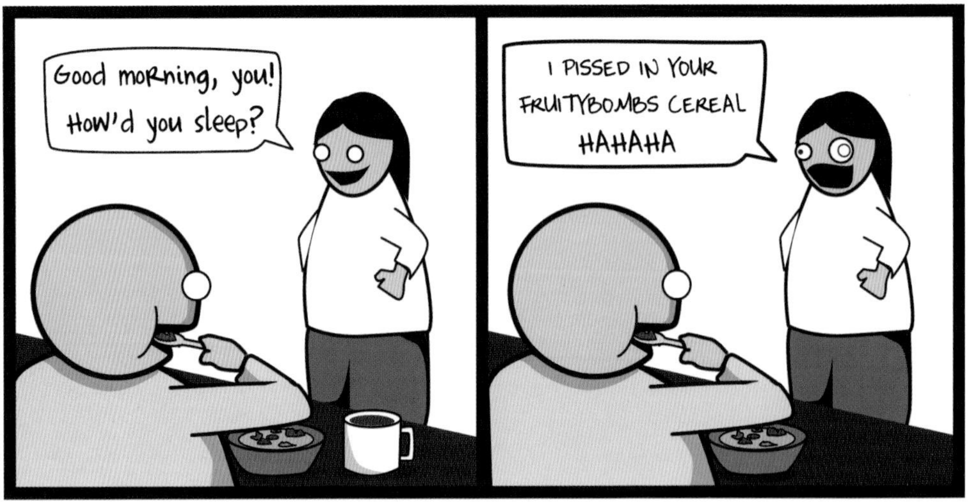
Good morning, you! How'd you sleep?
I PISSED IN YOUR FRUITYBOMBS CEREAL HAHAHA

WITH WITHOUT

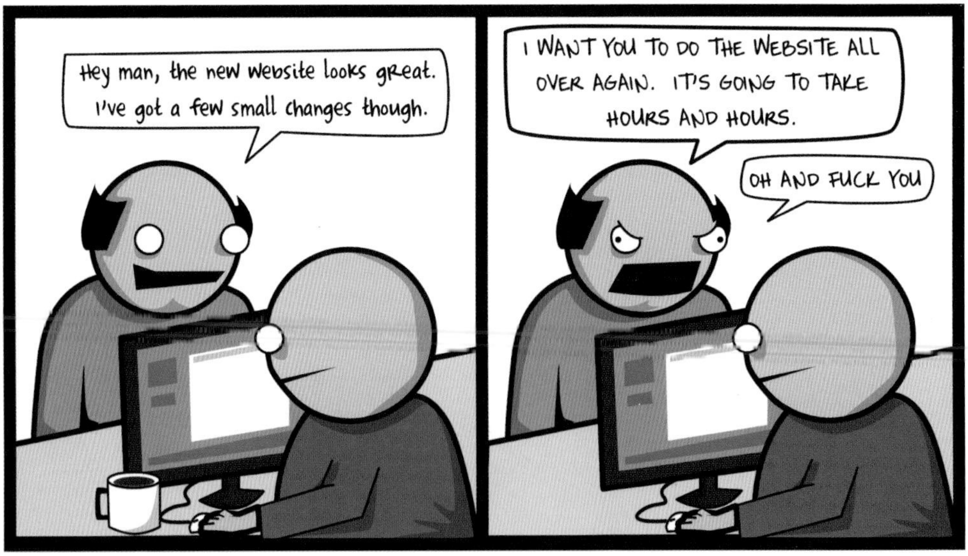
Hey man, the new website looks great. I've got a few small changes though.
I WANT YOU TO DO THE WEBSITE ALL OVER AGAIN. IT'S GOING TO TAKE HOURS AND HOURS.
OH AND FUCK YOU

WITHOUT   WITH

WITHOUT   WITH

The 10 Types of Crappy Interviewees

The over-dresser

The Under-dresser

The Stench

I put on a gallon of my favorite cologne: Kalvin Clein's "Desperation"

COUGH WHEEEZE COUGH

The Talker

I just wanted to know if you ... Wait ... ok hang on ... I just ... ... can I get a word in here?

So when I'm not studying foreign languages and nuclear physics, I bench press giant pieces of meat in order to fine tune my physique. When my arms get tired I take a few steaks off the pile and devour them. Impressive, huh? Did I mention I can juggle live animals? It's quite a sight, especially when I do it with a bunch of pissed off wolverines. You can check my references if you'd like, although it's just a bunch of my friends pretending to be previous employers.
  I think jobs are neat! I'd totally love to have one. I'm reliable and my mom said I could borrow her van to drive to work. I'm also gifted at...

The Mute

If you could describe your dream job, what would it be?

lots of money, i guess. and free nachos.

What? Speak up!

squeak
Can I get back to you on that one?

The Bullshi**er

How many years experience do you have building websites?

Well, I've social media'd awareness campaigns for my web 2.0 social meetspace. It's all about community and branding, you know?

The Trash Talker

On your resume it says you quit your last job due to "personal conflicts," can you tell me more about that?

Oh don't even get me started! My boss was a water balloon of a douchebag—a doucheballoon! haha! My co-workers? Inferior douchebaglets. Technically I was "fired," but I was planning to quit anyway to find a job that would appreciate my genius.

The Apologizer

Thanks for coming on such short notice

Why don't we start by you telling me a bit about yourself

Do you prefer working solo or on a team?

I'm sorry!

I'm so sorry!

OH GOD I'M SORRY!

The Nervous Twitcher

So here at Boyd's Toast we're looking for a designer who can really make things pop. Ideally someone with an eye for...

clickety click click click click
clickety click click clickety
click click clickety click click
click clickety click click
clickety click
click click click click clickety
click click click click
click click clickety click

The Appeaser

I'll do anything you want. I'll agree with everything you say. I'll excessively use your name in conversation and act excited about everything. Want me to eat this stapler? I'll do it, and by God I'll like it.

8 Ways To Tell If Your Loved One Plan To Eat You

1. Fattening you up

You're not leaving this table, young lady, until you finish 18 more doughnuts!

2. Asking for unusual favors

Would you mind cleaning the fireplace in the nude?

3. Slipping strange objects into the shower

shampoo

A YUM STEAK SAUCE

4. Swapping out all your clothes with butcher paper

5. Playing strange party games

6. Sneaking vegetables into the bathtub

7. Setting traps

8. Trying to "sample the goods" while you sleep

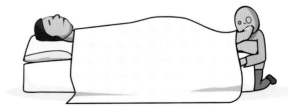

FAILED HUGS

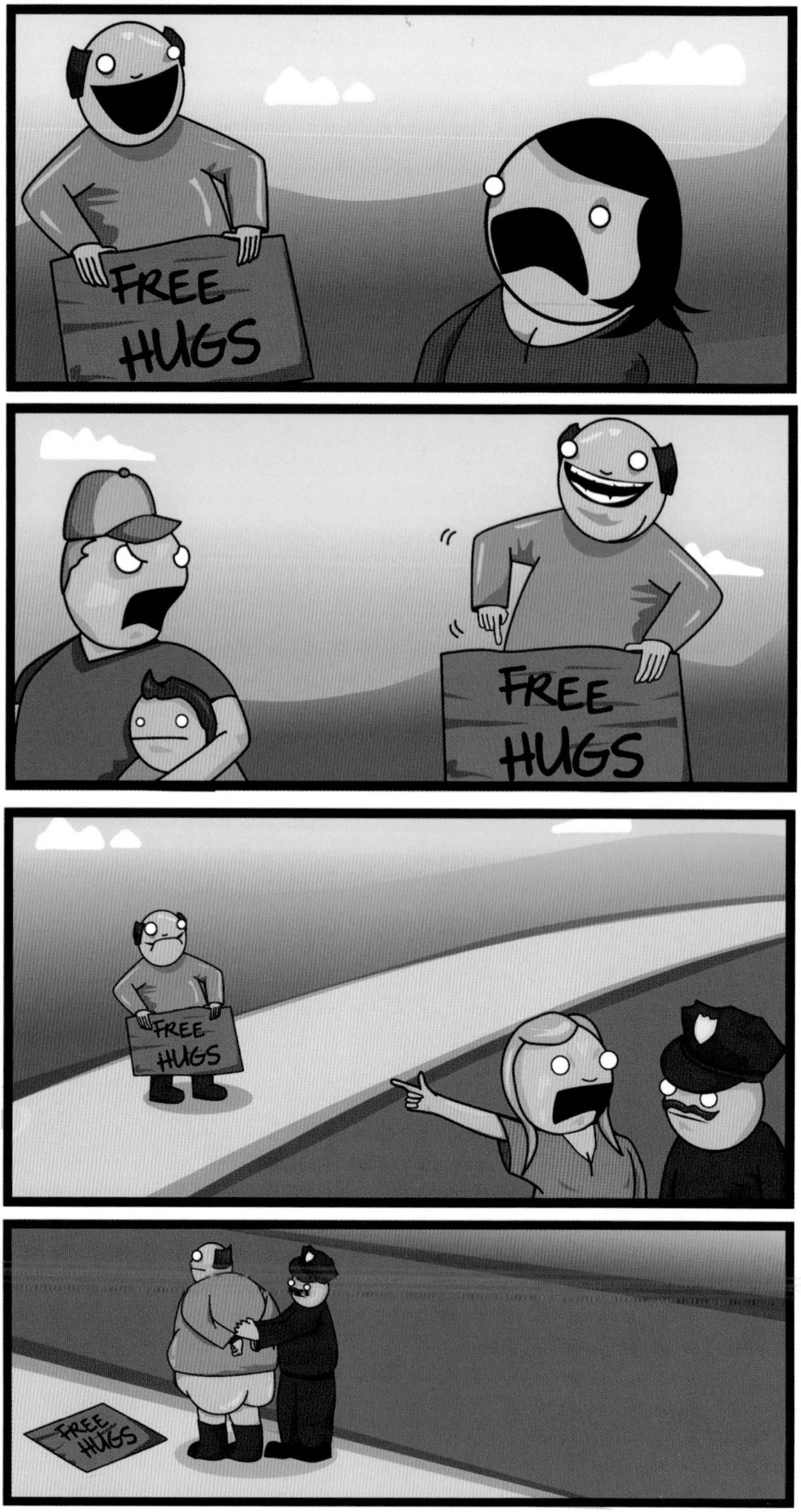
FREE HUGS
FREE HUGS
FREE HUGS
FREE HUGS

HOW TO *TRACK, HUNT, AND KILL* A UNICORN

1 OBSERVE

Unicorns leave a trail of happiness behind them.

Watch for newborn babies, happy couples, and tears of joy. If you see them, a unicorn is probably nearby.

2 TASTE

When a unicorn becomes relaxed, it craps out sherbet ice cream. If you spot a pile, it means you're close.

3 ENTRAP

Once spotted, set up a perimeter of claymores.

FRONT TOWARD UNICORN

Ensure proper spacing between claymores; you'll want to entrap the unicorn in a blast zone that'll splatter it straight to hell.

4 PRE-HEAT

If the unicorn survives the claymores, torch it with a flamethrower.

This will not only slow the unicorn down, but improve the flavor of the unicorn for later on!

5 THE KILL

The best way to take down a unicorn is with your mouth.

1. Run   2. Bite   3. Enjoy!

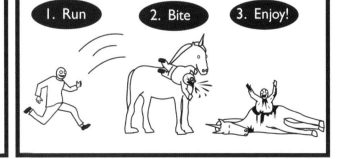

6 Reasons Bacon is Better than True Love

1. True love only happens once in a lifetime. Bacon can happen seven times a day, if you want it to.

2. Bacon you can keep in the fridge. True love you cannot.

3. Love is fleeting, but bacon stays in your arteries for all eternity.

4. It will always be there for you.

5. Bacon won't divorce you over a little misunderstanding.

6. Bacon does not nag or complain.

how to BUILD A CAMPFIRE
AND NOT LOOK LIKE AN ASSHOLE

1. GATHER STUFF

TINDER Tiny little sticks, dry grass, paper, or handfuls of human hair.

KINDLING Bigger sticks, but not too big. Roughly penis-sized.

LOGS Make sure they're dry. If you cannot find any logs, use dead animals or break the legs off the neighbor's furniture.

2. DIG A HOLE

DIG A SMALL FIRE PIT AND SURROUND IT WITH ROCKS.

If you run into a mixture of wood and tuxedos, you may have chosen a bad place to dig. Find another campsite.

3. BUILD A TEEPEE

START WITH THE TINDER AND BUILD A LITTLE TEEPEE. ADD THE KINDLING AROUND THAT TO BUILD A LARGER TEEPEE.

Keep an opening on the downwind side.

If you can't build a teepee or it keeps falling over, go find a nice lake and drown yourself in it because you are completely worthless.

4. BUILD A LOG CABIN

STACK THE LOGS AROUND THE TEEPEE TO CREATE A LITTLE CABIN.

 If you have any dead squirrels handy, feel free to dress them up like people to make the cabin feel more cozy.

5. LIGHT IT

 STICK A MATCH IN THE OPENING IN YOUR TEEPEE AND LIGHT THE TINDER.

If you smell burnt flesh and/or hear your loved ones screaming, you have not lit the campfire properly. Get another match and try again.

The 7 Types of Crappy  AIRLINE PASSENGERS

The Lonely

The Sleep Trappers

The Bigg'un

The GasBag

The Baby

The Elbow'ean Bonaparte

Conqueror of the armrest

The Giant Carry-on

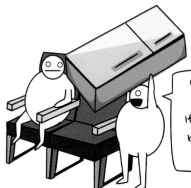

How A Web Design
Goes Straight To Hell

Everything is cool in the beginning.

The client communicates their needs. You set expectations.

Enthusiasm and excitement all 'round.

The client shows you their current website.

You both laugh at how terrible it is.

You re-design the website.

It looks nice and works well.
This is the high point of the design.

Just a few "minor" changes.

So this design is perfect, but I'm the CEO so I feel obligated to make changes to feel like I've done my job properly.

Also, I'll use phrases like "user experience" and "conversion oriented" to sound smart even though I barely know how to use a computer.

Could you make the design "pop" a bit more? It needs to be more edgy. It doesn't quite feel right. *

*Author's note: Clients have actually said all these things to me. To this day I still don't know what "pop" or "edgy" mean in regards to web design. I also don't know how to design websites based on someone else's feelings.

Minor changes start to add up.
Soon they become not-so-minor.

So I thought about it, and we definitely want to switch the font back to Comic Sans. Also, can you make a lens flare? Those are very web 2.0.

One other thing: The site definitely needs to be less "liney." When I look at it, all I see is lines. Can you do that? *

*Author's note: A client actually said this to me. The design had no horizontal rules or lines of any kind; they were referring to the rectangular shape created by things such as <div> or <p> tags.

The client gets others involved.
"Looks great, but I want to get feedback from my friend, co-workers, uncle, pet hamster, etc."

I've looped my mother into this conversation. She designed a bake sale flyer back in 1982, so you could say she has an "eye" for design. *

The design you put together needs some brighter colors; it's too gloomy. Perhaps a little pink? Throw in a kitten, too. EVERYONE LOVES KITTENS!

*Author's note: I actually had a client include their mother in the design process so she could provide feedback and criticism.

All hope is lost.
You begin to fantasize about other careers, like someone who digs ditches for a living or gives sponge baths to the elderly.

OK so my dog, Miffles, is a big deal.
He's basically the most important part of my life. I want you to add "stream of consciousness" copy to the web page, where it's like Miffles is talking to the user. I'll send you a few pages of narration of what Miffles is probably thinking about, such as "I love tasty treats!" and "Hello! Welcome to my website! I am a dog and you should shake my paw! LOL" *

*Author's note: I did not make this up—a client actually made this request. I've never come closer to braining someone with a cinder block as I did that day.

You are no longer a web designer.

You are now a mouse cursor inside a graphics program which the client can control by speaking, emailing, and instant messaging.

*Author's note: I once had a client take my design and start revising it themselves in Photoshop. They would then send me updated versions of how they felt it should look. After the 13th revision I fired the client.

An abomination is born.

The client has completely forgotten that they hired *you*, the web designer, to build them a great product. If you were an engineer designing the turbine of a commercial airplane, would they interfere then, I wonder?

6 REASONS
MAN NIPPLES
ARE AWESOME

STORAGE

NIPPLES ARE A GREAT PLACE TO HANG YOUR TOOLS!

NIPPLES CAN TELL THE TEMPERATURE

Hmmm...my nipples are pointed towards the heavens.

I'd say that puts us at about 28 degrees fahrenheit with possible snow showers in the early evening.

WILDERNESS SAFETY!

BY SHOWING YOUR NIPPLES, YOU CAN TRICK PREDATORS
INTO THINKING YOU HAVE COMPOUND EYES

 =

HOW YOU LOOK

HOW A PREDATOR SEES YOU

NAVIGATION

NIPPLES CAN GUIDE YOU WHEN YOU'RE LOST

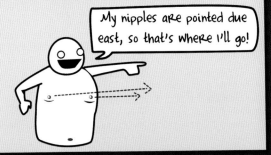

IN A SEA OF CHEST HAIR,

A MAN'S NIPPLES CAN HELP WOMEN FIND HIS PENIS IN THE DARK

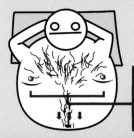

HALVE THE DISTANCE BETWEEN THE NIPPLES, THEN HEAD DUE SOUTH FOR SEXY TIMES!

NIPPLES ARE THE NORTH STAR OF A MAN'S BODY

LAUNDRY

WITH A NICE PAIR OF MAN NIPPLES, DRYING THE LINENS HAS NEVER BEEN EASIER!

Six Types *of* Crappy Hugs

The Crusher

Mismatched Heights

The Way-Too-Long Hug

The Man Hug

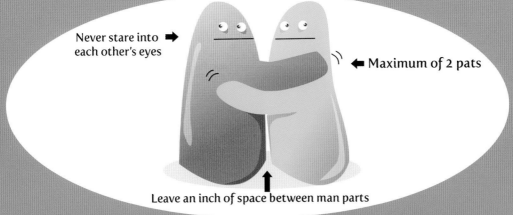

Never stare into each other's eyes ➡

⬅ Maximum of 2 pats

⬆ Leave an inch of space between man parts

Unwanted Kiss

The Let's-Get-This-Over-With Hug

8 WAYS TO IMPROVE YOUR HOME USING A HUMAN CORPSE

HAVE A SPARE DEAD BODY? DON'T THROW IT OUT!

① Brighten up the Christmas tree with a garland made of human teeth

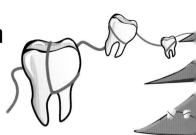

② Decapitated heads make great chew toys!

HOT TIP
Hollow out the eye sockets and fill them with peanut butter

MEGA CHUNK PEANUT BUTTER

③ The Ribcage   **④**

Strain Pasta   **OR**   Use it as a gift basket to welcome the new neighbors

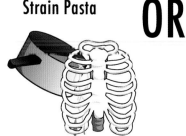

(5) Dress up your pets and be the talk of the town!  +  =

(6) Spice things up in bed with lingerie made from human entrails

(7) Handy storage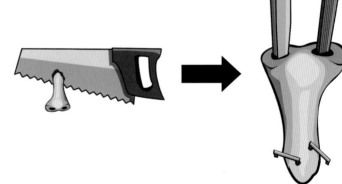

(8) Protect your kids from harmful UV rays: Create a fashionable "skin suit"

7 Reasons to Keep Your
Tyrannosaur
Off Crack Cocaine

1. He won't be able to sit through a long movie.

2. Afternoon walks in the park can be difficult.

3. He won't appreciate fine art.

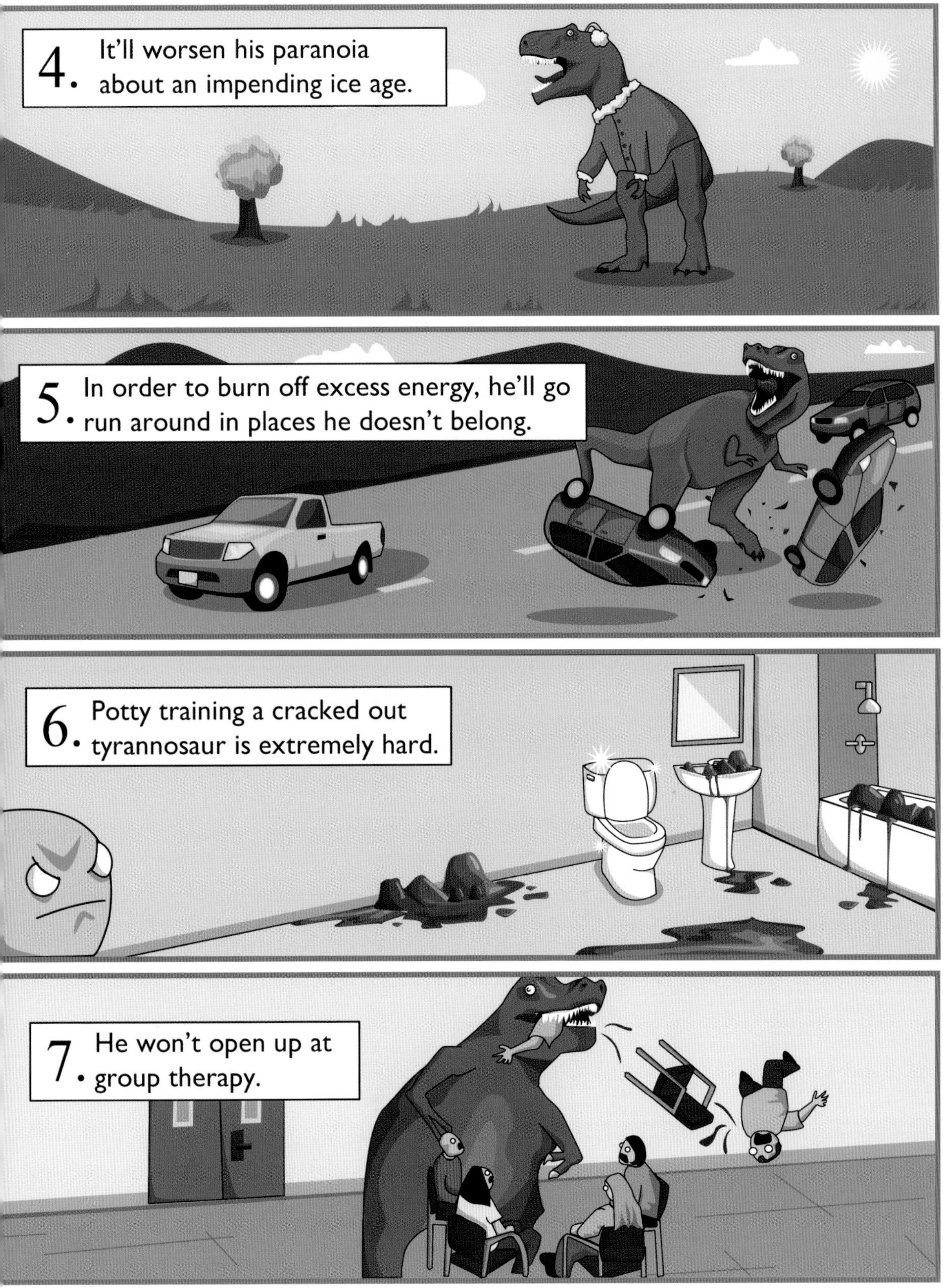
4. It'll worsen his paranoia about an impending ice age.
5. In order to burn off excess energy, he'll go run around in places he doesn't belong.
6. Potty training a cracked out tyrannosaur is extremely hard.
7. He won't open up at group therapy.

Why
Nikola Tesla
is the most awesome geek
who ever lived

One hundred years ago a genius by the name of Nikola Tesla ushered humanity into a second industrial revolution. He is considered the father of modern electricity.

It all started with his **cat.**

An animal lover, Tesla first became interested in electricity when his childhood cat zapped him with static.

> I think when I grow up I want to be a poet, or maybe I'll play the Ukulele and enchant the World with song.

SHOOOM!

> Holy thunderbags! Screw the ukulele, my destiny lies in electricity! Thanks Raiden Cat!

Tesla began his career in Austria, but later moved to the US where he invented a variety of things we still use today. These include:

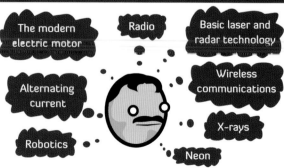

The modern electric motor

Radio

Basic laser and radar technology

Alternating current

Wireless communications

X-rays

Robotics

Neon

A t 28, Tesla was hired by Thomas Edison. Edison's motors and generators needed an upgrade, so he offered Tesla the modern equivalent of a million dollars to re-design them.

After Tesla finished and asked for payment, Edison laughed him off.

Tesla immediately quit and got a job digging ditches in order to make ends meet, meanwhile working on his AC electrical system.

Alternating current (AC) was Tesla's answer to Edison's direct current (DC). These systems are a means of transferring electricity from one place to another.

★ Edison's DC VS Tesla's AC ★

DC's dumb, lazy electrons could only travel in one direction.

AC's clever, zippy electrons travel in both directions.

DC required very thick cables and needed a large power plant every square mile in order to meet the world's energy needs.

AC used thinner wires, provided more voltage, and could easily be transmitted over long distances. All homes today use Tesla's AC system.

This made Edison rather...

Cranky, so he ran a smear campaign to discredit AC. He claimed it was too dangerous for home use, and to prove it Edison publicly electrocuted cats and dogs using AC.

He even electrocuted a live elephant.

In short:

Thomas Edison = Massive Dumptruck of Stinky Penises

I n the end, Tesla's system won the war of the currents and is what the entire world uses today.

I win! Go suck on a light bulb you fat little weasel.

bleeaaaaarggghhh!

C ompared to Tesla, most people's brains operate on the same level as a brain-damaged spider monkey.

This is you.

W hy? Because Tesla spoke **eight** languages: Most of us can barely speak two. ➡️ English, French, Serbian, Italian, Latin, German, Hungarian, and Czech.

▶ He could memorize entire books and recite them at will.
Most of us can't even remember our passwords.

▶ His photographic memory enabled him to visualize complex devices in his head and then build them without ever writing anything down. ➡️

Most of us only spend time visualizing things like greasy sandwiches and naked women.

U nfortunately, this also contributed to Tesla being utterly batshit insane. He often hallucinated, heard voices, and could not differentiate his imagination from reality.

Hey look! An ion quark defibrillator! I could build that with an allen wrench and an old can of porkchop soup.

Hey look! A bear burping in a bikini! Looks like SOMEONE is ready for summer to arrive! LOL

BRAP BRAP BRAAA BLORCH BRAP!

Earthquakes are a naturally occurring phenomenon, unless you happen to be roommates with Nikola Tesla. While living in NYC, he discovered the resonant frequency of the earth—something that scientists weren't able to confirm until 60 years later. Using this, he created an "earthquake machine." After turning it on, the machine nearly demolished his apartment building and the surrounding block had he not smashed it with a sledge hammer.

He also designed a "death ray," which supposedly could destroy thousands of airplanes from hundreds of miles away. Had Tesla possessed an evil bone in his body, he probably could have figured out a way to screw up the earth's rotation and send us all into the sun to fry like squealing little sausages.

BAH HAHAHAAAA. I WILL SPLIT THE EARTH IN TWO

oR mebbe just tuRn a big-ass wateR-fall into some seRious electRojuice

The first hydroelectric plant was built by Tesla at Niagara Falls.

When Tesla got bored, he did things like creating 130 foot (40 meters) long bolts of lightning in his front yard.

He still holds the world record for the longest bolt of man-made lightning.

Tesla coils were featured in the 1996 video game *Command & Conquer: Red Alert* as a defense structure used by the Soviets.

Tesla Coil = Photon Cannon for Commies

Speaking of socialism...

Free energy for the entire planet was one of Tesla's final offerings to the world. In his Colorado laboratory, Tesla built a device which could transmit electricity wirelessly for 26 miles. Using this technology, he received funding from J.P. Morgan and built the Wardenclyffe Tower.

This tower would provide free energy and communications for the entire planet. Morgan, upon discovering Tesla's plans to provide free energy, shut the project down believing there was no financial gain to the idea.

In short: { Nikola Tesla was an insanely brilliant geek who changed the world for the better. }

6 WAYS TO FIGHT A CRACK WHORE

IF SPOTTED, PUT SOMETHING OVER YOUR HEAD AND MAKE LOUD NOISES. THIS WILL TRICK HER INTO THINKING YOU ARE A LARGE PREDATOR.

HOO HOO!
HRRNNGGG

JABBA JABBA
HRRNNGGG

NEVER RUN FROM A CRACK WHORE. THEY ARE UNMATCHED IN SPEED AND *WILL* CATCH UP.

DO NOT LET A CRACK WHORE BITE YOU. ONCE LOCKED DOWN, THEIR POWERFUL JAWS ARE IMPOSSIBLE TO REMOVE.

THROW A FEW DOLLARS ON THE GROUND. WHILE SHE'S DISTRACTED, UNLEASH A WICKED BODY SLAM.

BEING HIGH ON CRACK WILL MAKE HER PAIN TOLERANCE VERY HIGH, SO APPLY A SLEEPER HOLD IF YOU CAN TO END THE FIGHT.

PUT SOMETHING SHINY ON YOUR SHOES. WHEN SHE BENDS OVER TO LOOK AT IT, CRANE KICK HER IN THE FACE.

FAILED EXPERIMENT

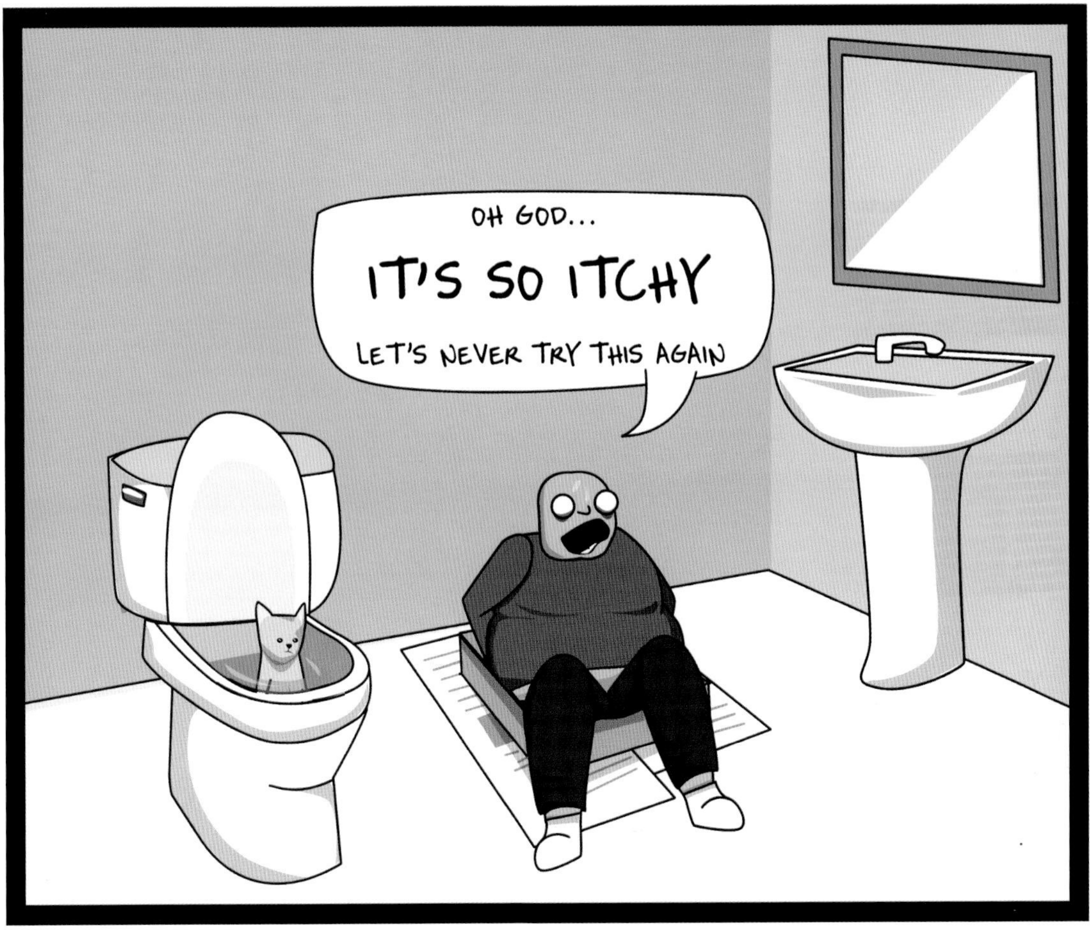
OH GOD...
IT'S SO ITCHY
LET'S NEVER TRY THIS AGAIN

8 Things
Raccoons Will Try to Eat
(But Can't)

1

Slow-moving Farm Equipment

2

HTML Code

3

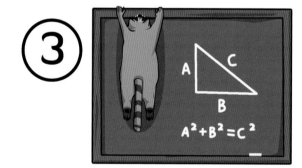

A²+B²=C²

Mathematical Theorems

4

Lightning Storms

5 Other Raccoons

6 Distant Planets

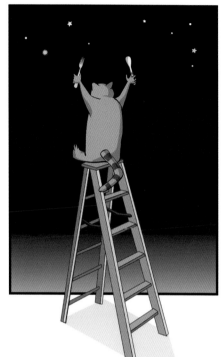

7 Flightless Birds

8 Heavy Sleepers

THE THREE PHASES
OF OWNING A COMPUTER

 **PHASE 1:**
THE HONEYMOON

YOUR NEW COMPUTER IS CAPABLE OF ANYTHING
INCLUDING SPLITTING THE ATOM AND PRODUCING BAKED GOODS.

YOU HAVE NO IDEA WHAT A 4.9 MEGAWATT RAM PULSE DRIVE IS, BUT
YOU HAVE ONE AND YOUR FRIENDS DON'T   (WHICH IS ALL THAT MATTERS).

IF ONLY YOUR TESTICLES WERE MADE OF USB,
YOU'D MAKE LOVE TO YOUR NEW COMPUTER EVERY NIGHT.

PHASE 2:
THE COMFORTABLE PHASE

YOU AND YOUR COMPUTER ARE NOW BFFs 4 LIFE.
YOU KNOW ALL ITS SECRETS, AND IT KNOWS ALL YOURS.
(INCLUDING YOUR DIRTY PORN HABITS.)

WATCHING SOMEONE ELSE USE YOUR COMPUTER
IS LIKE WATCHING A DRUNK ORANGUTAN SOLVE A RUBIX CUBE.

THEY HAVE NO IDEA WHAT THEY'RE DOING AND YOU WISH THEY'D
JUST HAND YOU THE DAMN THING SO YOU CAN DO IT YOURSELF.

PHASE 3:
BEHOLD, THE DINOSAUR

THE COMPUTER IS CONSTANTLY "THINKING,"
EVEN WHEN NOT IN USE. ABOUT WHAT, I WONDER?

DON'T OPEN THE CASE:
IT'S LIKE PEERING INTO THE DUSTY
RECTUM OF A 2000-YEAR-OLD MUMMY.

THE FANS NEVER STOP GROANING AND GRINDING
WHO KNEW COMPUTERS COULD GET INDIGESTION?

NOTHING WORKS RIGHT
SO YOU BLAME YOUR COMPUTER FOR ALL LIFE'S PROBLEMS.

 OR, BLAME THE PERSON WHO MADE THE OS!

→ BILL GATES IS GENGHIS KHAN WITH A PROGRAMMING DEGREE.

→ LINUS TORVALDS IS A DIRTY COMMIE.

→ STEVE JOBS IS A COCKWAFFLE IN A TURTLENECK.

BOOTING UP
GIVES YOU AN IDEA OF HOW LONG AN ICE AGE CAN LAST.

YOU FEAR POWERING THE COMPUTER OFF
BECAUSE IT MAY NOT TURN ON AGAIN.

THE MOUSE AND KEYBOARD HAVE A NICE GREASY SHEEN.
SAVE THE GREASE—USE IT TO STYLE YOUR HAIR OR COOK SAUSAGES!

YOUR DESKTOP
LOOKS LIKE SOMEONE VOMITED UP EVERY
PDF, ZIP FILE, AND JPEG ON THE INTERNET.

Why it would suck to live next to a VOLCANO

Ice cream socials are OUT.

Pyroclastic flow can be hard on a marriage.

No social life.

Relaxing can be difficult.

Playing tag is OUT.

THE 8 PHASES OF FLYING

1. The Sit Down

As you board, you pray your seat isn't next to the wrong kind of passenger.

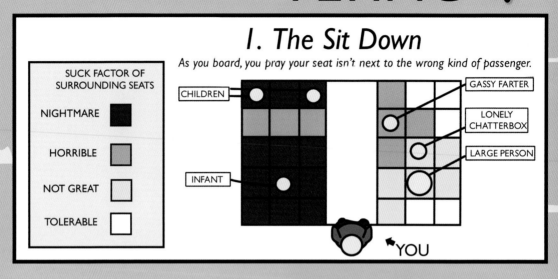

SUCK FACTOR OF SURROUNDING SEATS

NIGHTMARE

HORRIBLE

NOT GREAT

TOLERABLE

CHILDREN

INFANT

GASSY FARTER

LONELY CHATTERBOX

LARGE PERSON

YOU

2. Safety Briefing

Someone with a painted-on smile gets up and puts on a show about how to survive the impossible.

In the event of a mid-air collision and your mangled body is blasted through one of the turbines, you'll find a few wet naps under your seat to apply to your wounds.

3. Warmup Round

When the first drink cart comes by, you're usually feeling pretty good. You might even chat up a passenger.

Holy bubbling beverages! You drink ginger ale too!?

You bet your sweet ass I do!

4. Movie Time!

You don an inaudible headset and settle down to watch a movie you'd never watch unless you were stuck on an airplane.

PIG HARD 2
PIG HARDER

5. The Meal

Airline food is only enjoyable because it keeps your mind occupied for a little while. You eat for the sport of it, basically.

You want the bloated porkflesh or the floaty-fishy-fish?

6. Turbulence

Without Turbulence

I'm sleepy

Sandwiches are neat

With Turbulence

I'M TOO YOUNG TO DIE! I REALLY WANT TO HOLD THIS DUDE'S HAND RIGHT NOW

OH GOD OH GOD OH GOD OH GOD JUST LET ME LIVE THIS ONE TIME AND I PROMISE TO NEVER LOOK AT INTERNET PORN AGAIN

7. The Aching Desert

Dehydrated, cramped, and aching—
a long flight can transform man into beast.

HOUR 1	HOUR 6	HOUR 12

8. Landing

It's usually during landing that you begin to question the abilities of your pilot.

Your perception of the pilot during the flight	Your perception of the pilot during landing

Roger that, steady as a rock. Tango alpha mango salsa. Over.

WOOOOOO I'M FLYIN AIRPLANE BUMPITY BUMP DERR BAHAHA

4 REASONS TO CARRY A SHOVEL AT ALL TIMES

I. GOOD FOR SOLVING PROBLEMS

2. INSTANT BACKYARD FUN

3. SETTLE ANY DEBATE

1. NO MORE LONG LINES AT THE SUPERMARKET

How to use a semicolon
The most feared punctuation on earth

Why
What's the point of a semicolon?

The most common way to use a semicolon is to connect two independent clauses. For example:

> " *The ice cream truck man drove by my house today.*
> *He had big hairy knuckles.* "

The two statements are separated by a period.
If read aloud, it would go something like this:

> " *The ice cream truck man drove by my house today.*
> *take a breath*
> *He had big hairy knuckles.* "

With a semicolon, however, it would sound like this:

> " *The ice cream truck man drove by my house today;*
> *he had big hairy knuckles.* "

Basically what we did was eliminate the pause between the two statements without using words such as *and, but, nor,* or *yet.*

How
How do I use a semicolon?

If you have two independent clauses, meaning they could stand alone as their own sentences, it's OK to use a semicolon. For example:

> " *My aunt also had hairy knuckles; she loved to wash and comb them.* "

This is an independent clause, meaning it could stand alone as a complete sentence.

This is also an independent clause; it could exist without being attached to its predecessor.

KNUCKLE
SHAMPOO

LET YOUR
KNUCKLE HAIR
SHINE!

Don't

Don't use it with conjunctions.

Conjunctions are words like *and, but, or, nor, for, so,* and *yet.*

> " *My aunt's hairy knuckles are magnificent indeed, but I have no desire to stroke them.* "

A comma is used because there's a *but* separating the two clauses.

When

When should I use a semicolon?

> " *I gnaw on old car tires; it strengthens my jaw so I'll be better conditioned for bear combat.* "

Use a semicolon when you want to form a bond between two statements, typically when they are related to or contrast with one another. In the example above, the relationship between gnawing on tires and combatting bears is strengthened by using a semicolon.

> " *I fought the bear and won. Also, I never kiss plague rats on the mouth.* "

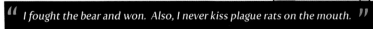

HERE is ok to kiss

NEVER kiss here

In this sentence, your victory against the bear does not need to be connected to the plague rat, so a period is used.

Pause

Both bears and semicolons have pause.

Comma
(brief pause)

Semicolon
(moderate pause)

I'm pretty sure bologna is made out of cow elbows, but I ♥ it anyway.

222...222...22

Period
(complete stop)

Internal

Use a semicolon to connect sentences that contain internal punctuation.

I've got all these commas! How can we ever be together without forming a run-on sentence?!

Nothing can stop true love. Use a semicolon, you fool!

❝ *When dinosaurs agree on something, they'll often high five one another; dinosaurs are all about high fives.* ❞

If you'd used a comma in this sentence it would have resulted in a comma splice. If you'd used a period you'd lose the connection between the two clauses.

Super

Use a semicolon as a super-comma.

> *While searching for a good place to get a unicorn burger, I traveled to Seattle, Washington; Tokyo, Japan; and London, England.*

Use a semicolon if you need to make a list of items that are separated with a comma. This often occurs when listing locations, names, dates, and descriptions.

The most enchanting meat on earth comes from the thighs of a unicorn.

Mayonnaise made me the man I am today!

> *My favorite people include Samuel Slaughterjaws, a famous unicorn hunter; my uncle Wilford, a world champion at mayonnaise eating contests; and Nikola Tesla, the most awesome dude to ever fire a lightning bolt at an angry peasant.*

The semicolon enables you to list and describe all three characters in the same sentence.

The End.

> *Using a semicolon isn't hard; I once saw a party gorilla do it.*

Twenty Things
Worth Knowing About
Beer

The ancient Babylonians were the first to brew.

In fact, they took their beer so seriously, if you brewed a bad batch your punishment was to be drowned in it.

CAMEL BEER
MADE FROM 100% CAMEL POOP
HIGH FIBER! OK TASTE!

Beer is mostly composed of

Water

which isn't particularly interesting.

What *is* interesting, however, is that the water in certain regions were originally better suited to making certain types of beer.

Dublin's mineral-rich hard water, for example, was great for making Stouts such as Guinness.

You don't need special water, however, for a

Beer Tsunami!

In 1814,

a brewery tank containing 3,500 barrels of beer ruptured causing a tidal wave of beer through a London Parish. Two houses were demolished and nine people died.

In the middle ages clean water was often difficult to find. Many people chose to drink beer instead because the alcohol made it safer than water.

Perhaps they went to Valhalla

Vikings believed that a giant goat whose udders provided an endless supply of beer was waiting for them in Valhalla (viking heaven).

Sad Beer   Happy Beer

↑ ↑ ↑
Store it upright

I ♥ goat titty beer

This minimizes oxidation and contamination from the cap.

How Beer is Made
(In a nutshell)

First, **Malted Barley** is mixed with hot water, creating the "mash," a mushy oatmeal-like substance. Next, a sugary liquid called

Wort
Pronounced "wert"

is drained off.

The **Hops** come after that.

The hops are boiled with the wort to add bitterness, flavor, and aroma.

Hops are the flower of a vine that is a member of the marijuana family.

(But you can't smoke hops, so don't try.)

Next, **Yeast** is mixed with the hopped wort and left to ferment.

The yeast converts sugar into

ethanol and **carbon dioxide**

Ethanol is what gets you drunk.

Not everyone likes being drunk.

CO_2 adds bubbles to the beer.

Everyone likes bubbles.

Most beer falls into two categories

Ales

When the yeast ferments at higher temperatures and stays at the surface, it produces an ale.

Super toasty yeast sits at the top

Popular ales include Pale Ale, Stout, Porter, Hefeweizen, Blonde, IPA, Belgian Ale, and Amber.

Lagers

When it ferments at a lower temperature and does not float at the surface, it produces a lager.

Not-so-toasty yeast floats around

Popular lagers include Pilsner, Bock, Marzen, Helles, Doppelbok, and Dunkel.

Lastly,

It sits and ferments for a few weeks until it's put into a bottle, keg, or water balloon and

Voila!

A beer is born.

"We're outta brewskis, mang pull this thing over"

"omg need moar"

Pilgrims on the Mayflower
stopped at Plymouth Rock rather than continuing on to Virginia because they ran out of beer.

PROHIBITION
in the US lasted
13 years
10 months
19 days
17 hours
32.5 minutes

Afterwards,
President Roosevelt said:

"What America needs now is a drink"

What he really meant:

"let's get wasted mothafuckaaaas"

You can categorize beer in many ways
One way is mouthfeel (how it feels in your mouth).

flavor
aroma
alcohol content

"good golly gumdrops! it's like having a slip 'n slide in my mouth!"

"Mine feels like having a dead porcupine in my mouth"

Cenosillicaphobia
is fear of an empty glass. This is why we recommend double-fisting.

How you get drunk
After drinking booze, the alcohol is absorbed into your stomach and small intestine and eventually enters the bloodstream, where it is carried throughout the body.

Drinking on an empty stomach makes you get drunk faster because the alcohol is absorbed more quickly.

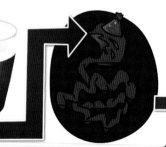

Your body eliminates the alcohol through urination, breathing it out, and by breaking it down in the liver.

Your body can break down about one drink an hour.

When you drink faster than your body can process, you get drunk.

 Next, we'll take a ride on the booze choo-choo train through your **Brain!**

First it hits the cerebral cortex. This makes you more talkative and less inhibited.

Can I just say one thing? I find panda bears to be very arousing.

> "All right, brain, I don't like you and you don't like me—so let's just do this and I'll get back to killing you with beer."
> —Homer Simpson

When the alcohol reaches the hippocampus of your brain, it causes memory loss and exaggerated emotions.

HEY, F U! MISTER "I'M NOT AROUSED BY PANDAS" THINKS HE'S SO HIGH AND MIGHTY. imma beat your ass

> "You can't be a real country unless you have a beer and an airline - it helps if you have some kind of a football team, or some nuclear weapons, but at the very least you need a beer."
> —Frank Zappa

The cerebellum keeps you balanced. When alcohol hits it, you lose coordination.

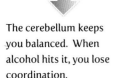

I fell down... Help me up so I can punch you in the face and maybe go vomit on the couch.

If the alcohol reaches your medula, you're in trouble. The medula regulates activities which you do not have to think about, like regulating your heart rate and breathing.

RIP

Here lies Jimbo.

He had too many brewskis in his medula oblongata.

> "Not all chemicals are bad. Without chemicals such as hydrogen and oxygen, for example, there would be no way to make water, a vital ingredient in beer."
> —Dave Barry

Speaking of death ...

Michael Jackson died on August 30, 2007

Michael Jackson was an author and beer critic who helped start a renaissance of interest in beer in the 70s.

7 Reasons
to avoid going to a
night club

The Line

First, you get to stand outside with a bunch of douchebags sporting collared shirts and spikey hair.

The Cover

The Line at the Bar

"Dancing"

By dancing, I mean getting mashed around in a giant crowd of sweat and boners.

I can't dance so I'll just shuffle my arms a lot and thrust my groin at you!

OMG attention! I love it!

HOLLA!

You say holla?! I say Holla too! We have one thing in common so let's dwell on that all night as a reason for liking each other!

Making Conversation

OONTZ OONTZ OONTZ OONTZ

Hey there, I noticed your drink was empty. Can I buy you one more?

WHAT?! I CAN'T HEAR Y-

I SAID... CAN I BUY YOU ONE MORE?

YOU KISSED A WILD BOAR?

YES, ONE MORE. CAN I BUY YOU A SHOT?

YOU HAVEN'T HAD YOUR SHOTS?

The Women

How a female clubber wants to be perceived by men

How she actually looks

Sexy Temptress

✔ Dark tan
✔ Gallons of makeup
✔ Skimpy clothes
✔ Sexy, but unattainable

Slutty Oompa Loompa

The Men

How a male clubber wants to be perceived by women

How he actually looks

Lord of the club

Rich, sophisticated, and the object of every woman's desire.

Retarded penis monster

BLEAAAAAARG I AM BONERBEAST LET ME BUY U DRINKS

Broke, lives outside the city in some town you've never heard of, and is very, very lonely.

HOW DIFFERENT AGE GROUPS CELEBRATE HALLOWEEN

Infants and Toddlers

Their parents dress them up in some horribly embarrassing outfit and they're too young to know better or fight back.

Children

Their Halloween involves excitedly running around the neighborhood and collecting a stockpile of sugar high–inducing treats.

Halloween will never be as awesome as this.

Teenagers

They try to go trick or treating and get yelled at by stingy parents, so typically they end up sitting at home complaining about how lame Halloween is.

Young Adults

They dress up like hookers, get wasted, and screw each other.

Adults

They go trick or treating with the kids they conceived at a drunken Halloween party years earlier.

Seniors

They stay home and give out crappy candy.

How to Suck at  Messaging

"Sexting"
A favorite among those who are too afraid to flirt in person

☑ 1 new message

OMG been thinkin about u baby. ur tittays are so neat

Over-abbreviating
Talking like this cuts your IQ in half with a samurai sword

☑ 1 new message

lets g2 prty 2nite n pt sm nachos in ur mouth lol! u knw wr flyin 2day on skypork airlines gnna b rad!! amirite?!

Initiate Lengthy, Complex Conversations

☑ 1 new message

What are your hopes and dreams for your life? Do beautiful sunsets make you weep with tears of awesome? Tell me everything in excruciating detail.

Mass Texts

☑ 1 new message

Merry Xmas! I love you guys so much I'm sending you all an identical text message instead of actually calling you

Pointless Texts
Especially popular amongst bored teenagers

☑ 1 new message

sup

Drunk Texting

☑ 1 new message

hey jerry FU. ur a crappy manager and i think ur wife is hot. hahah cu at work tomorrow a-hole

Not Proofreading
One letter can make all the difference

☑ 1 new message

would you mind raping the yard when u get home? the leaves are really starting to pile up

8 WAYS TO PREPARE YOUR PETS FOR WAR

$$\begin{array}{r} \text{Mini jet turbine} \\ \text{Butcher knife} \\ + \ \text{Parakeet} \\ \hline = \ \text{Supersonic Flying Death Blade} \end{array}$$

Arm all kittens with samurai swords.

Cats are natural predators. Combine these instincts with ancient weaponry and you'll have an unstoppable soldier.

The speed and agility of a bunny makes them ideal for special ops.

Disguise your dog as a panzer tank.

The enemy will not know the difference.

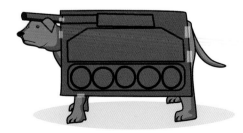

Use hamsters to sneak grenades into enemy territory.*

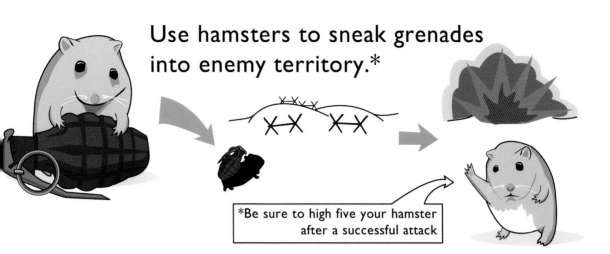

*Be sure to high five your hamster after a successful attack

Cats lack compassion and empathy, which makes them ideal for leadership. Promote your kitties to generals as soon as you can.

Hamsters love 50 calibers.

frrp!

Use biological weapons:
Feed your dog enough junk food and he'll fart lethal nerve gas.

Why I'd Rather be punched in the testicles than call customer service

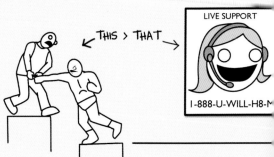

← THIS > THAT →

LIVE SUPPORT

1-888-U-WILL-H8-M

→ First you have to find the phone number

Usually the number is near a picture of a beautiful woman wearing a headset.

The person they want you to think you're calling

The person you are REALLY calling

Once on the line, you can speak your selection. Wow! What a timesaver!

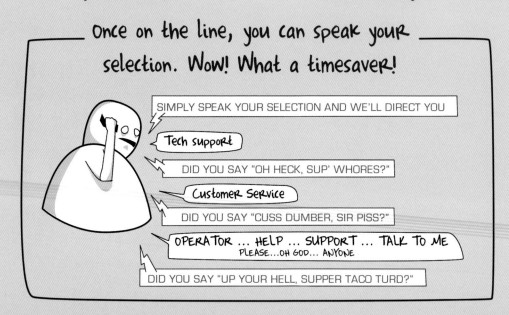

SIMPLY SPEAK YOUR SELECTION AND WE'LL DIRECT YOU

Tech support

DID YOU SAY "OH HECK, SUP' WHORES?"

Customer Service

DID YOU SAY "CUSS DUMBER, SIR PISS?"

OPERATOR ... HELP ... SUPPORT ... TALK TO ME
PLEASE...OH GOD... ANYONE

DID YOU SAY "UP YOUR HELL, SUPPER TACO TURD?"

You give up on speaking your selection and opt to dial it instead.

FOR BILLING, PRESS 1
FOR SALES, PRESS 2
FOR JIMBO'S SUPER FUN JOKE LINE, PRESS 3
TO HEAR OUR HOURS OF OPERATION, PRESS
UP UP DOWN DOWN LEFT RIGHT LEFT RIGHT B A
TO HEAR WAVES CRASHING, PRESS 4...

Sometime later...

FOR THE NEAREST TACO TRUCK, PRESS 9,345,233
FOR TECHNICAL SUPPORT, PRESS 9,345,234

Now it's time for HOLD MUSIC!

The worst part about being on hold isn't the music. It's when every minute or so they dim the music to play an automated message.

This constantly teases you into thinking you're about to get a live person.

ONCE MORE
YOU OPEN THE DOOR
AND YOU'RE HERE
IN MY HEART
AND MY HEART WILL GO ONNNNN-

THANK YOU FOR HOLDING
YOUR CALL IS VERY IMPORTANT TO US.
SO IMPORTANT, IN FACT, WE'LL CONTINUE TO KEEP YOU ON HOLD
SO THAT BY THE TIME YOU REACH A REAL PERSON YOUR MOOD WILL
HAVE BECOME AS FOUL AND BLACK AS SATAN'S STOOL SAMPLE.

A human being!

You eventually reach a real live person! Not a robot! They're made of carbon! They have things like body hair and a pituitary gland! ⟶

Hello sir! Can I get your first name, phone number, address, date of birth, favorite planet in the solar system, and least favorite African mammal. I won't actually log this information, mind you, so you'll have to repeat it to every other operator I forward you to.

My name is Matthew Inman.
Saturn is OK, I guess. I hate water buffalo because they just sit around and chew leaves all day instead of contributing to the welfare of the jungle like all the other animals.
Also, their nasty buffalo farts are depleting the ozone layer.

Nice to meet you Mickel Inderman! How can I help you today?

My phone is busted. It's plugged into the wall and fully charged but it won't turn on.

Won't turn ON? I'm sorry, my department only handles phones that won't turn OFF. Please hold while I redirect you.

MORE HOLD MUSIC!

for the love of God play another song

♪ AND YOU'RE HERE ♫
IN MY HEART
AND MY HEART WILL GO ON AND ONNNNNN

Hello Sir! How can I help you today?

My phone is busted. It's plugged into the wall and fully charged but it won't turn on.

Have you pressed the power button?

Yes, of course

Have you tried pressing it <u>really</u> hard?

Yes, although I really don't think that makes a diff-

PLEASE HOLD while I forward you to an advanced support specialist!

PLEASE NO MORE. CELINE, I BEG YOU

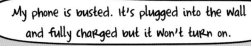

♪ AND YOU'RE HERE IN MY HEART AND MY HEART WILL GO ON AND ONNNNNN ♫

Dumb questions ensue

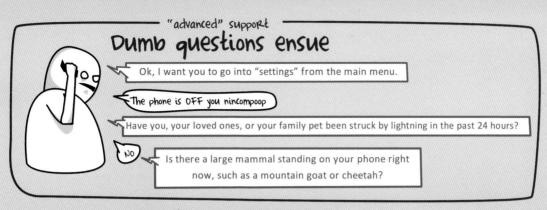

Ok, I want you to go into "settings" from the main menu.

The phone is OFF you nincompoop

Have you, your loved ones, or your family pet been struck by lightning in the past 24 hours?

NO

Is there a large mammal standing on your phone right now, such as a mountain goat or cheetah?

Replacement time!

Why fix it when they can just send you another disposable piece of crap?

Well sir, it sounds like you need a replacment phone. Our records show that your warranty expired approximately 11 minutes ago, so you'll have to pay for another.

However, your account indicates that you've been a loyal customer for 14 years. This entitles you to a $2 off coupon on the cheapest, crappiest phone we sell!

Allow me to redirect you to our sales department

♫ AND MY HEART WILL GO ON AND ONNNNNNNN ♫

YOUR HEART IS GOING TO END UP ON A PIKE IN MY FRONT YARD, CELINE

I WILL FIND OUT WHERE YOU SLEEP

YOU WILL SUFFER AS I HAVE SUFFERED

$ The Sales Dept $

It's amazing how being on commission affects someone's attitude

Hello sir, Welcome to Sales! My name is Skippy McSkipperSkip and I'm the cheeriest guy you'll ever talk to!

the sky is gonna open up i will murder you a thousand times over

Ha ha! That sounds GREAT sir! Would you be interested in becoming a platinum premium member? It's the PERFECT plan for a champ like yourself.

your intestines will be my jump rope .... your skull - my urinal

5 Ways to Lose Weight
like a
★ CHAMP ★

1. Eat a tapeworm sandwich

2. Supersonic Bulimia: **Induce vomiting via an F-15 barrel roll**

3. Lose a limb

I said chop, god damnit so I can be pretty!

4. Intensify your daily jog by kicking a bear in the balls

5. Live in the desert for a few months and do the "lizards and dirt" diet

Finally, no more love handles!

HOW TO NOT SELL SOMETHING
TO MY GENERATION

FIVE REASONS
PIGS
ARE MORE AWESOME
THAN YOU

My name is Bill!
I like the Roof cuz it get me closer to outer space

Pigs are smart

Within a few weeks of being born a pig will recognize its own name.

God damnit Bill!
I told you to stay off the Roof!

A Roof is no place for unruly swine.

Pigs are ranked #4 in animal intelligence;
they are only outranked by elephants, dolphins, and chimps.

Quadratic equations are 2 EZ
Let's go split the atom using a chemistry kit and that squirrel over there.

PLZ don't turn me into a nuke

nuclear proliferation makes me sad :(

Pigs can ea

A pig can (and will) eat pretty much anything.

yes i am pig

Dood We're outta rotten nac
Let's go eat some snakes!

porkmang

This includes:

Meat, tree bark, grass	Dead armadillos
Fruits & Veggies	Rotting buffalo
Slow-moving farmers	Other pigs (really)

Pigs can scream
The sound made by a jet engine is around 113 decibels.
A pig can scream at 115 decibels.

zzzzz...zzz

BOO!

SQUEEEEAAALLL!

Pigs are fast

A pig can run a seven-minute mile.

(1.6 km in 7 minutes)

Last, but not least:
A pig's orgasm lasts <u>30 minutes</u>.

Human "O-face"   Pig "O-face"

I did it!

10 minutes later...

10 minutes later...

Why I'd Rather

~~Re-absorb the poop into my body~~ ~~Walk to the ends of the earth~~

hold it in for a year

~~turn my backpack into a makeshift colostomy bag~~ ~~crap in the bushes~~

than use a Porta Potty

The Primitive

We live in a modern age of mobile technology, lunar missions, and fruit rollups. Despite this, the porta potty stands unevolved as a bucket of shit in a field.

This = This

The Pressure

Time you normally take to do your business
× Number of people waiting in line
= Must poop at 5x speed

The Sight

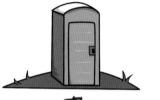

Even though it's like making eye contact with Satan himself, you can't help peering down into the bowl.

Inside the bowl you'll see all the crimes of humanity splattered into a pile, which you then have to dangle your privates over.

The Smell

The scent they add to the toilet bowl does not make it better. Instead, it makes it smell like shit dipped in honey.

The same applies to lighting a match, which makes poop smell like it's been roasted in an oven.

The Splishy Splash

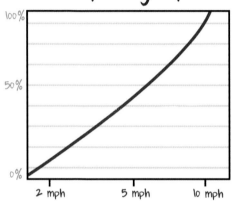

Chances of blue water splashing up and hitting you

100%

50%

0%

2 mph   5 mph   10 mph

Velocity at which your feces is propelled into the porta potty

The Vertigo

Porta potties have a mysterious power which makes you feel like you're going to fall inside the bowl.

It's similar to when you're standing on a cliff and feel like you're being pulled over the edge.

Airplane toilets also have this power; their mighty flush makes you fearful of being sucked through a shit-pipe and blown into the clouds.

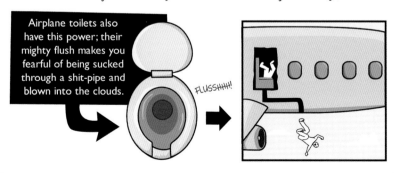

FLUSSHHH!

10 Things That Bears Love

Overweight Hikers

Wrestlers
(more fun to maul)

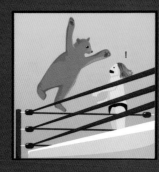

Drunks

Fabric Stores
(convenient camouflage)

Girl Scouts
(defenses are easy to infiltrate, plus free cookies after mauling)

Emergency Exit Rows
(more leg room)

Roller Coaster Photos

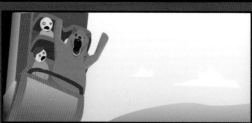

Petting Zoos

Boomboxes
(music for the slaughter)

Team-Building Exercises

Seventeen Things
Worth Knowing About Your → cat

Your cat's front paws have **five** toes

The back paws have **four**

Unless your cat is polydactyl.

Polydactyl means having extra toes. The high rate of polydactyl cats in Boston, USA has led people to refer to 8-toed cats as "Boston Thumb Cats."

Your cat purrs at the same frequency as an idling diesel engine.

This is around 26 purrs per second.

Guinea pigs, rabbits, squirrels, lemurs, elephants, and gorillas also purr.

Had your cat been born in ancient Egypt, the Egyptians may have used your kitty to protect crops from   rats and other vermin.

go away you dumb Rats

Had your cat stuck around in ancient Egypt for long enough, the Egyptians may have eventually come to worship your cat—even going so far as to mummify your kitty after death.

Your cat can see in the dark. Cats can see at one-sixth the light level required for human vision.

Do not spend good money on these; they are totally unnecessary.

Your cat cannot taste things that are sweet.
The taste buds of a cat cannot detect sugar.

← Kitties are not impressed by cupcakes.

CLUMPING FTW

Originally kitty litter was made from sand, but in 1948 it was discovered that clay was more absorbent.

Nikola Tesla was zapped by his cat.

As a child Nikola Tesla was inspired to understand the secrets of electricity after being shocked by static electricity from his cat.

Isaac Newton invented the cat flap door.

MRRRROOWWW

First you want out, now you want in. MAKE UP YOUR DAMN MIND, KITTY!

Famous Cat Haters

I HATE CATS!

Dwight D. Eisenhower
Commander of US forces
in Europe during WWII

OMG me too. They give
my armies itchy eyes.

Adolf Hitler
Commander of the Nazi
forces during WWII

Famous Cat Lovers

I love my kitty.
Let's end this war and start
a kitty ranch together.

OK LOL

Robert E. Lee
Commander of the South
during the Civil War

Abraham Lincoln
Commander of the North
during the Civil War

Your cat's ears can hear ultrasonic sounds.

Rodents use these sounds to communicate. Your cat can hear them but dogs and humans cannot.

Let's poop on something expensive

WORD

Speaking of Abe...

President Lincoln kept four cats in the White House.

Your cat can run at
30 miles per hour!
(48 KPH)

Your cat uses whiskers to gauge whether or not they can fit through an opening.

Furthermore, your cat's collarbone does not connect to any other bones but instead sits buried in muscle.

This makes it easier for your cat to squeeze through tight spots.

Your cat purrs continuously...

...by flowing air past the voice box during both inhalation and exhalation.

A kitty stole my gold medal :(

Usain Bolt
100 meter world
record holder
 27 MPH

Domestic housecat
 30 MPH

Cheetah
75 MPH

Without Taurine, your cat would go blind.

Taurine is an amino acid that most animals produce on their own, but cats require it in their diet. Don't worry, it's in your cat food.

Taurine is also an ingredient in most energy drinks*

Energy
Cow Juice

*but this doesn't mean you should ever give these to your cat

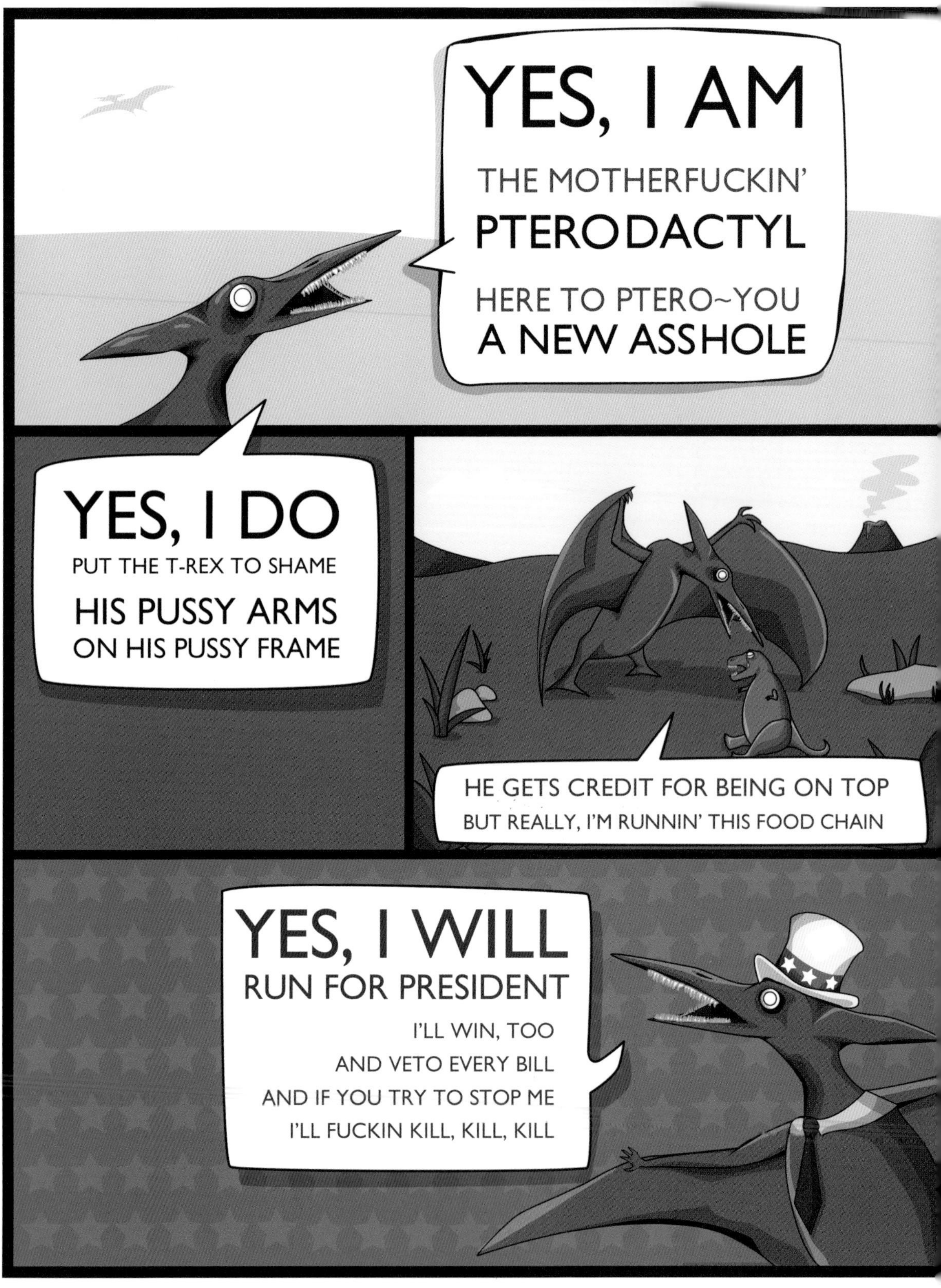
YES, I AM
THE MOTHERFUCKIN' PTERODACTYL
HERE TO PTERO~YOU A NEW ASSHOLE
YES, I DO
PUT THE T-REX TO SHAME
HIS PUSSY ARMS ON HIS PUSSY FRAME
HE GETS CREDIT FOR BEING ON TOP
BUT REALLY, I'M RUNNIN' THIS FOOD CHAIN
YES, I WILL
RUN FOR PRESIDENT
I'LL WIN, TOO
AND VETO EVERY BILL
AND IF YOU TRY TO STOP ME
I'LL FUCKIN KILL, KILL, KILL

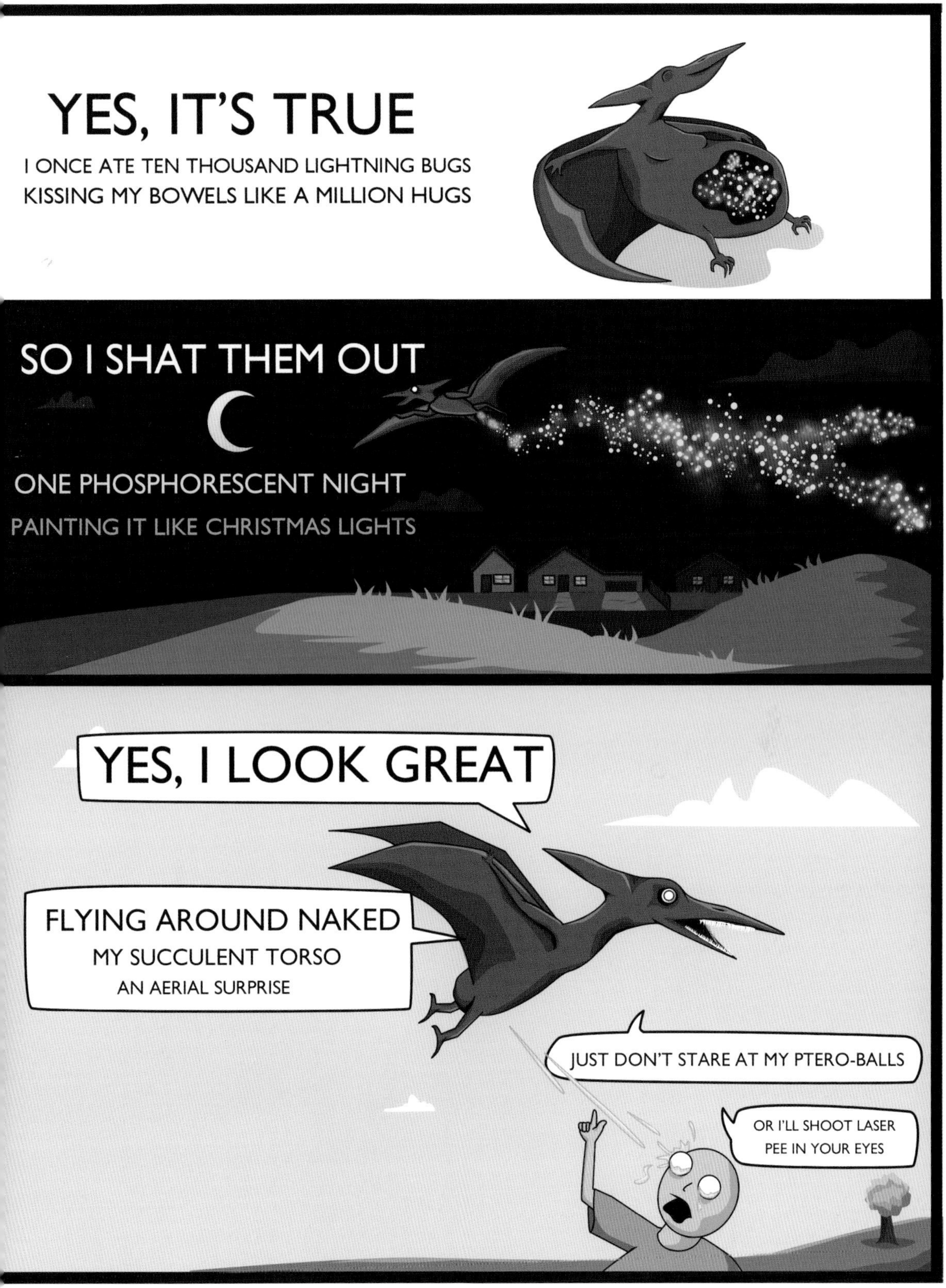

YES, IT'S TRUE
I ONCE ATE TEN THOUSAND LIGHTNING BUGS
KISSING MY BOWELS LIKE A MILLION HUGS
SO I SHAT THEM OUT
ONE PHOSPHORESCENT NIGHT
PAINTING IT LIKE CHRISTMAS LIGHTS
YES, I LOOK GREAT
FLYING AROUND NAKED
MY SUCCULENT TORSO
AN AERIAL SURPRISE
JUST DON'T STARE AT MY PTERO-BALLS
OR I'LL SHOOT LASER PEE IN YOUR EYES

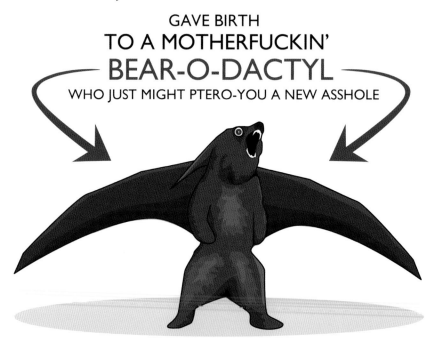

YES, THAT BEAR

GAVE BIRTH
TO A MOTHERFUCKIN'
BEAR-O-DACTYL
WHO JUST MIGHT PTERO-YOU A NEW ASSHOLE

SO BEWARE, MOTHERFUCKERS, BEWARE.

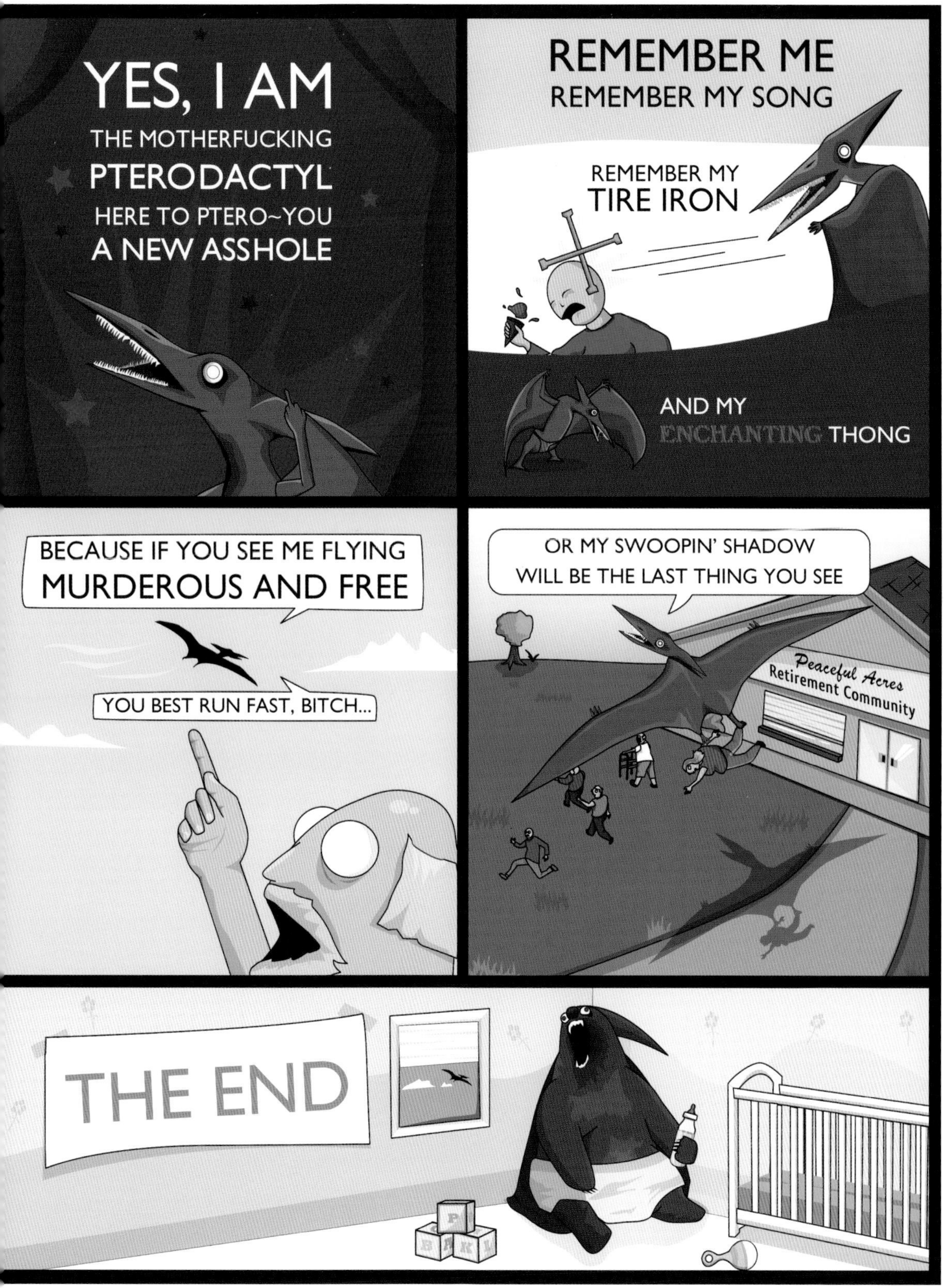

YES, I AM
THE MOTHERFUCKING
PTERODACTYL
HERE TO PTERO~YOU
A NEW ASSHOLE
REMEMBER ME
REMEMBER MY SONG
REMEMBER MY
TIRE IRON
AND MY
ENCHANTING THONG
BECAUSE IF YOU SEE ME FLYING
MURDEROUS AND FREE
YOU BEST RUN FAST, BITCH...
OR MY SWOOPIN' SHADOW
WILL BE THE LAST THING YOU SEE
Peaceful Acres
Retirement Community
THE END

HOW TO MAKE A MOVIE TRAILER
TOTALLY AWSUMMMM!!

FIRST,
TELL THE VIEWER THAT THIS MOVIE WILL SHAKE THE VERY FOUNDATIONS OF THEIR HUMANITY

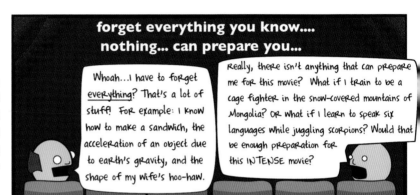

forget everything you know....
nothing... can prepare you...

Whoah...I have to forget everything? That's a lot of stuff! For example: I know how to make a sandwich, the acceleration of an object due to earth's gravity, and the shape of my wife's hoo-haw.

Really, there isn't anything that can prepare me for this movie? What if I train to be a cage fighter in the snow-covered mountains of Mongolia? Or what if I learn to speak six languages while juggling scorpions? Would that be enough preparation for this INTENSE movie?

NEXT,
SHOW SOMETHING HAPPY AND NORMAL

Bill had everything a man could want: an expensive car, a great job, and a family who loved him. Until one day...

THEN,
DRAGON-KICK IT IN THE MOUTH

... IT WAS ALL TAKEN FROM HIM

NEXT,
TURN UP THE INTENSITY KNOB TO SHIT-YEAH

THEY TOOK EVERYTHING FROM ME
I WILL HAVE VENGEANCE

CHANGE
FRAMES EVERY HALF SECOND

IMAGINE YOUR AUDIENCE AS A
BUNCH OF ADHD TEENAGERS
RIDING A MASSIVE SUGAR HIGH

INTRODUCE
THE HERO OF YOUR STORY

SAY SOMETHING FOREBODING
THEN MAKE THE SCREEN GO BLACK
AND MAKE A LOUD BASS SOUND

SAY SOMETHING CLEVER
FOLLOWED BY AN EXPLOSION

INTRODUCE
THE DIRECTOR

THEN,
DROP THE TITLE LIKE AN ATOM BOMB

Minor Differences

Grocery shopping while **full**

Grocery shopping while **hungry**

How you are perceived with
CAPSLOCK OFF

How you are perceived with
CAPSLOCK ON

MOTORISTS cutting each other off

Pedestrians cutting each other off

cereal WITH milk

cereal WITHOUT milk

With a smiley face :)

Without a smiley face

4 Reasons the Easter Bunny is a **Giant Asshole**

1 He deposits a lot more than Easter eggs.

2 He steals bedsheets and uses them for extreme sports, such as base jumping.

3 He thinks expensive high-def cables are delicious.

4 Easter eggs, if left to hatch, can be troublesome.

The **6 Phases** *of a* Tapeworm's Life

1. Everything's cool, then some asshole eats undercooked meat and turns your whole world upside down.

2. Fortunately, your new home offers a wondrous, unlimited supply of delicious food.

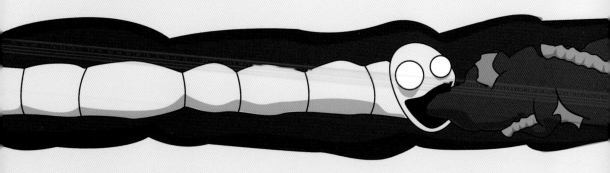

. Soon you become fat and lonely...

. ...so you shed parts of your body and make lots of friends.

. Then the asshole who got you here in the first place figures out something is wrong and starts taking tapeworm medication.

5. You die, and you are given a funeral without dignity, honor, or compassion.

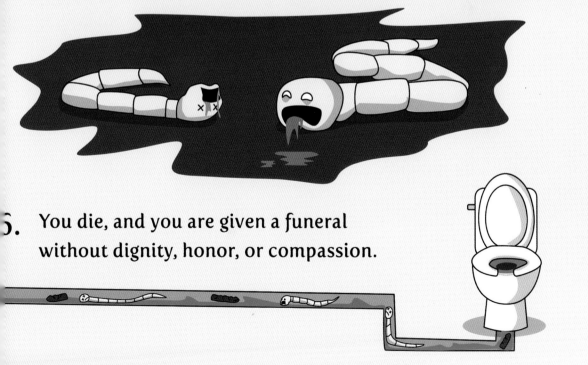

FAILED BUSINESS

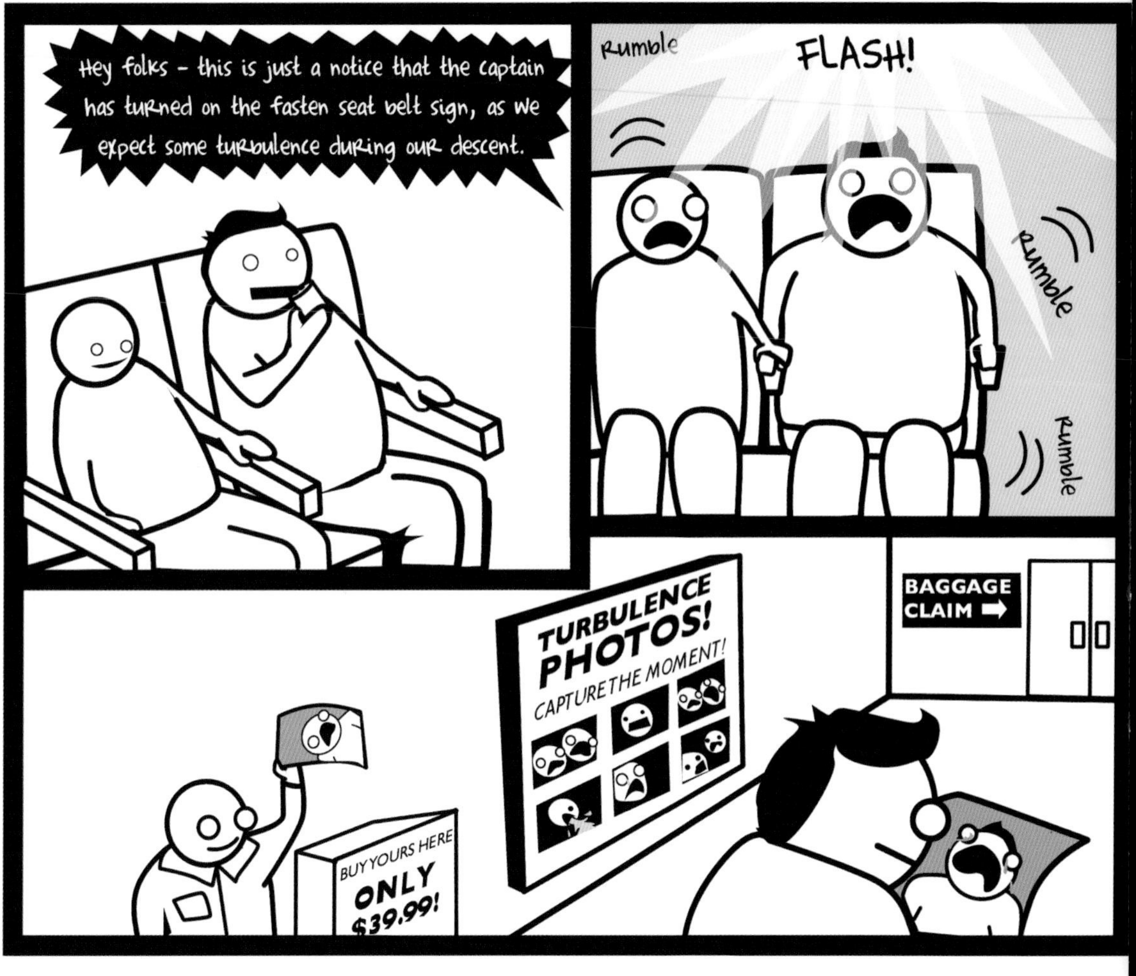

Hey folks - this is just a notice that the captain has turned on the fasten seat belt sign, as we expect some turbulence during our descent.
Rumble
FLASH!
Rumble
Rumble
TURBULENCE PHOTOS!
CAPTURE THE MOMENT!
BAGGAGE CLAIM
BUY YOURS HERE
ONLY $39.99!

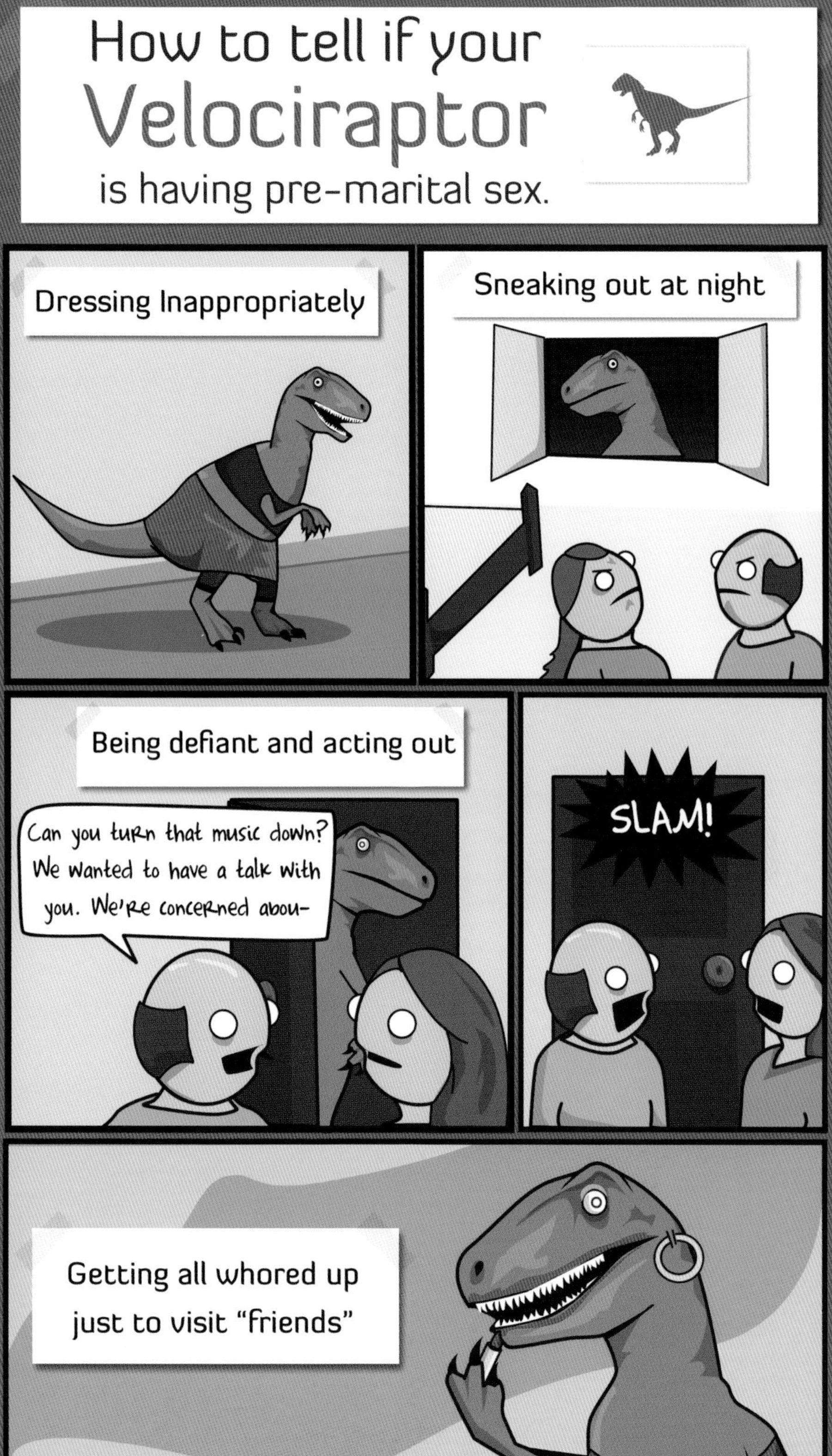
How to tell if your
Velociraptor
is having pre-marital sex.
Dressing Inappropriately
Sneaking out at night
Being defiant and acting out
Can you turn that music down? We wanted to have a talk with you. We're concerned abou-
SLAM!
Getting all whored up just to visit "friends"

The 8 Phases of Employment

1. Fear

plz hire me, I am tired of eating cardboard and dead mice to survive

2. Lies

I can do 1,000 pushups and when I pee diamonds come out

HOLY MOTHERF*NG SHIT -
Our company is AMAZING!
We invented the ballpoint pen, gravity, and everyone here is SO HAPPY

bossguy

3. Excitement and Wonder

I use fancy words to sound impressive. For example: In today's economy, we need to synergize ROI within the social tweet sphere.

OOOOOOOOOOOOOOOOOOH
ur so smart. I have much to learn.

bossman

4. Enthusiasm

I need you to work all weekend on this horrible list of tasks that I'm too lazy to do. Also, eat this magnificent cat turd.

You got it! Anything for you, mr. bossman!

bossdude

5. Doubt

Dear whatsyourface,

Drop everything you're doing and instead design software that will turn a PDF or ZIP file into a tasty meat sandwich.

-bossman

6. Disinterest

75 Unread Emails

- REPORT DUE NOW !!
- where are you?!
- URGENT - i need
- hello?

is due today

video - skateboard kitty

hurr hurrr huhuh hurrrr

7. Loathing

Today's economy depends on meat sandwiches in social media. It's all about the ROI!

bossperson

You're a f***ng retard

8. Jubilation

Screw this job, I'm quitting and stealing all your office supplies

Oh, and I'm the guy who's been stealing everyone's lunches out of the fridge for the past two years. Thanks for all the free sandwiches, a-holes!

15 (ish) Things Worth Knowing About Coffee

It all started with

Dancing Goats

Legend has it...

Ethiopian shepherds first noticed the effects of caffeine when they saw their goats appearing to become frisky and "dance" after eating coffee berries.

Originally,

Coffee was eaten. African tribes mixed coffee berries with fat which formed edible **energy balls!**

70% of the world consumes Arabica coffee, which is mild and aromatic. The remaining 30% drinks Robusta, which is more bitter-tasting but has 50% more caffeine than Arabica.

30% Robusta

70% Arabica

All coffee in the world grows in the

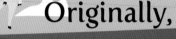

Bean Belt

The "Bean Belt" is a fancy word for the equator.

The rise of Islam

contributed greatly to the popularity of coffee. The religion prohibited drinking alcohol, but coffee was considered an acceptable drink.

In 1675, the King of England banned coffee houses, claiming they were places where people met to conspire against him.

NO COFFEE DRINKING

BY ORDER OF THE KING, COFFEE SHOPS ARE NOW DECREED TO BE "TERRORIST SLUMBER PARTIES"

George Washington invented instant coffee!

No I didn't. Don't just skim. Read the damn details. Do it or I'll cross the Delaware and crane kick you in the mouth.

A Belgian man living in Guatemala by the name of George Washington invented it in 1906.

Coffee grows on trees

They can grow to be up to 30 feet tall,
but are cultivated to be around 10 feet
(3 meters) tall for easy-picking.

This tree is ridiculous. I can't even reach.

Much better thx.

The bean is actually a seed inside of a *bright red berry.*

← here's a photo

chug! chug! chug!

Coffee is

the second most traded
commodity on earth.

Oil is the first.
Clearly humanity has a thing
for black drippy liquids.

Coffee Berries
are picked, dried, and
stripped down until all
that's left is a green bean.

POP!

Once shipped, the beans are roasted at around 500°F. After a few
minutes, the bean will "pop" and double in size. A few minutes after that,
the bean will "pop" once more. The second pop means the bean is done.

The bean is now ready to fulfill its destiny.

POP! (part 2)

I was destined for greatness, for I will
end up in someone's coffee cup and
make a boring task seem exciting!

Espresso: |e-spres-oh|

It's not a particular type of bean, roast, or blend.
Espresso is just a way that coffee is prepared:
shooting pressurized, hot water through finely ground coffee.

Caffè Latte

Foam

Tons o' Milk

Espresso

Mocha

Whipped Cream

Milk

Chocolate Syrup

Espresso

Cappuccino

Tons o' Foam

Milk

Espresso

Americano

Water

Espresso

Breve

Foam

Half & Half

Espresso

Espresso

(and nothin' else!)

(this is hardcore)

Espresso

I AM A WAR MACHINE!
BUT PLEASE DON'T MAKE MY
COFFEE TOO STRONG :(

Americano

The term "Americano" comes from American GIs during WWII.
They would order espresso with water to dilute the strong flavor.

Caffeine

How it works:

In your brain there's something called Adenosine and it only wants to hang out with certain receptors. When these two get together, you get drowsy.

 sup mang let's party!

I got my party hat on. let's rock this casserole

adenosine   adenosine receptor

When Caffeine shows up, it attaches to the receptors so that Adenosine cannot.

forget that guy he's a total square

i never liked him anyway

I am so lonely.

caffeine   adenosine receptor   adenosine

Your pituitary gland sees this and thinks there's an emergency, so it tells the adrenal glands to produce adrenaline.

In addition, caffeine bumps up your dopamine levels

I dunno WTF is going on up there, but it's a big deal 4 sure

imma give u an adrenaline sandwich k?

pituitary gland

The result?

A CAFFEINE HIGH

The End

THE END!

How To Use An Apostrophe

Is it plural?

Plural means more than one.

For Example:
I saw two **kittens** riding a goat.
Cats are great for transportation.

 → **DON'T**
USE AN APOSTROPHE

Two Exceptions

Is it a single letter word! For example:
There are two t's in "kittens."
Then it's OK, but you can also do this:
There are two "t"s in "kittens."

Is it a number or abbreviation?
For example:
**90's fashion was a bit awkward.
Just say no to hammer pants.**

Then do this:
**I attended college in the
late '90s and early 2000s.**

Is it indicating possession?  **USE**
AN APOSTROPHE

Possession means to own something.

For Example: Bob's hat was made out of jelly beans.

Is it plural and possessive? For Example:
*The **soldiers'** rifles were no match for Bob's
amazing lightning pants.*
Then put the apostrophe after the "s."

 **But Watch Out**

Unless It's a word that's already plural, such as
"children," then you'd write "children's."

Is it a contraction? ⟹ **USE**
AN APOSTROPHE

A contraction is when you omit a few letters. For example:

I (cannot ➡ can't) believe you fit that entire watermelon in your mouth!

I (do not ➡ don't) like putting honeybees in my underpants.

I (would not ➡ wouldn't) recommend scuba diving inside a volcano.

IT'S

1 **Are you trying to say "it is?"**
(or "it has")
For Example:

It's (it is) unusual to put crickets in your coffee, but I do it anyway.

It's (it has) been a fun day. We should go to the velociraptor petting zoo more often!

USE
AN APOSTROPHE

If you're unsure, try replacing *it's* with *it is*. If it sounds OK that way, use an apostrophe.

ITS

2 **Are you indicating possession?**  **DON'T**
USE AN APOSTROPHE

For Example:

The velociraptor is known for **its** cute, playful nature, but **its** inability to sing in key is unfortunate.

NAMES

Is it a possessive <u>and</u> plural name? **STICK IT**
AFTER THE "S"

For Example: **The Johnsons' moonwich recipe was very famous.**

In this case, you're referring to the entire Johnson family.

Is it a possessive name ending in "s?"

For Example:

Charles's rocketship allowed him to have lunch on the moon. **BOTH**
ARE ACCEPTABLE
JUST BE CONSISTENT

Charles' cat is always terrified during liftoff.

TO RECAP

Remember that most apostrophes are used for possessive nouns. So if a noun owns something, use an apostrophe:

Bob's *jellybean hat became sticky in the scorching sun.*

Or use it for contractions:

Bob's *going to the store to create a bacon hat instead.*

And if it's plural, don't use an apostrophe:
*Bacon **hats** do not melt and they smell wonderful.*

LASTLY
When in doubt

DON'T
USE AN APOSTROPHE

A POLAR BEAR'S GUIDE TO MAKING NEW FRIENDS

(IN 5 EASY STEPS)

People love surprises. Start things off right by showing up unexpectedly.

If they run away from you, it means they want to play. Chase them.

Party games are great for breaking the ice between bears and people. Drag someone to your cave for a game of "hot potato."

For added fun, pretend to be asleep near the cave entrance and watch them try to sneak past you. This game can last for days or even weeks!

Give big, warm hugs. If your new friend stops moving, you may have hugged too hard.
Find another one and try again.

FAILED WELCOME

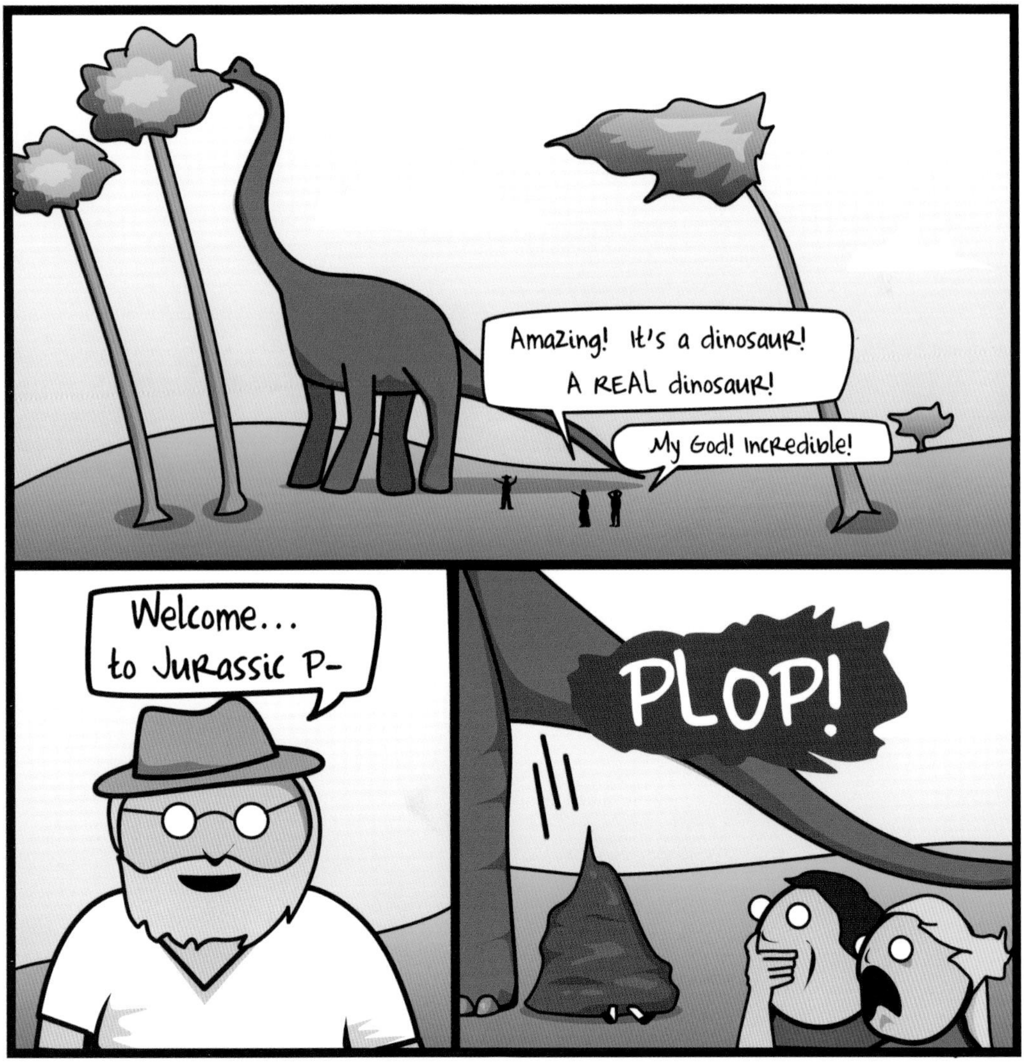
Amazing! It's a dinosaur! A REAL dinosaur!
My God! Incredible!
Welcome... to Jurassic P-
PLOP!

HOW EVERYTHING GOES TO HELL DURING A
ZOMBIE APOCALYPSE

IT ALL STARTS
WITH SOME A-HOLE SCIENTIST, DOING SHIT HE SHOULDN'T BE DOING.

> I know! Let's mix rabies with this old meatloaf and feed it to the gorilla!

NATURALLY

THE GORILLA BECOMES INFECTED.

SO INSTEAD OF SAY, LOCKING THE GORILLA UP IN QUARANTINE, HE DOES SOMETHING RETARDED LIKE TRYING TO TEACH IT HOW TO DO MATH.

> I believe in your potential, Coco.

ONCE BITTEN,
THE SCIENTIST IGNORES HIS SYMPTOMS FOR AS LONG AS POSSIBLE.

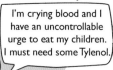

> I'm crying blood and I have an uncontrollable urge to eat my children. I must need some Tylenol.

TO THE HOSPITAL WE GO!

...WHERE A ZOMBIE IS BORN

ONCE AGAIN, QUARANTINE IS OUT OF THE QUESTION. INSTEAD, THE DOCTOR GETS WITHIN MAKE-OUT RANGE OF THE ZOMBIE TO EXAMINE HIM.

> Now hold still. If you're a good patient, I'll let you take a sucker from the bowl on your way out!

> Now Say AHHHH

AGGGHHHH
GRAAAAAGHHH AGGG!

> Atta boy!

YOU CAN IMAGINE
WHAT HAPPENS NEXT

mister fancy-ass doctor gets MAULED he then runs around the hospital biting, gnawing, and throwing up blood on his patients.
(like the asshole that he is)

SHORTLY THEREAFTER...

THE INFECTION SPREADS

WAY TO GO, DUMBASSES!

INMAN
MEDICAL CENTER

IF YOU FIND A LOVED ONE:

THE WRONG THING TO DO:

Barbara, I still love you—and nothing is more powerful than love. After I met you, my life was changed forev—

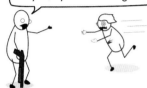

OH GOD
BARBARA, NO!

THE RIGHT THING TO DO:

I always hated "date night" LOL

PEOPLE START FLOCKING TO A SUPPOSED "SAFE ZONE"

BAHAHAHA

This is what zombies would say to that if they knew how to talk

THEIR TRIP DOES NOT END WELL.
THEY GET TURNED INTO HUMAN HAMBURGER MEAT.

THE SURVIVORS SEEK REFUGE
(AND DO A REALLY CRAPPY JOB AT IT)

FUN ZONE!

FOOD N' GUNS R' US

Let's hide in the one on the left. It's got a ball pit!

ONCE INSIDE, THEY SQUABBLE FIGHT AND BICKER

I'm in charge here!

No, I AM! You're overweight and have crappy aim!

OVER WHO GETS TO BE MAYOR OF "WE'RE-ALL-FUCKING SCREWED-VILLE"

MEANWHILE...

THE ZOMBIES PUSH THROUGH THEIR CRAPPY BARRICADE AND EAT THEM LIKE THE USELESS LITTLE BITCHES THAT THEY ARE.

← HE HAD THIS COMING.

OFFICIAL SCORE

ZOMBIES	1
HUMANS	FUCKALL

The 5 Phases of Caffeine Intake

1. Pre-caffeinated

DIE DIE DIE DIE

2. The first few sips
The magic begins!

3. The High

4. The Runs

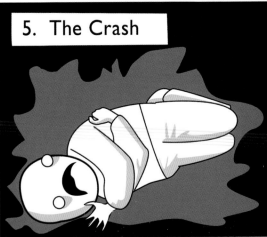

5. The Crash

PUNCHLINE ALIENS

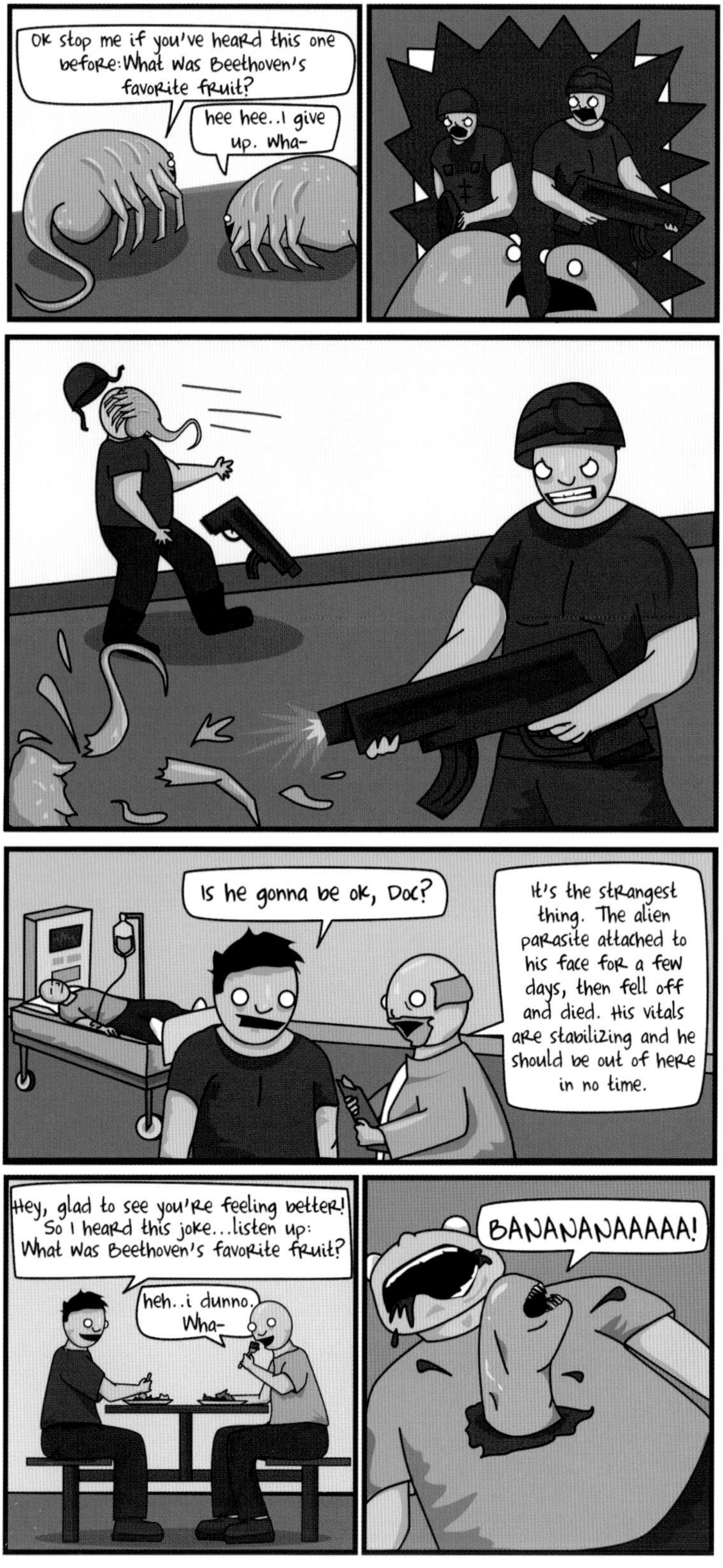

OK stop me if you've heard this one before: What was Beethoven's favorite fruit?
hee hee..I give up. Wha-
Is he gonna be ok, Doc?
It's the strangest thing. The alien parasite attached to his face for a few days, then fell off and died. His vitals are stabilizing and he should be out of here in no time.
Hey, glad to see you're feeling better! So I heard this joke...listen up: What was Beethoven's favorite fruit?
heh..i dunno. Wha-
BANANANAAAAA!

The 7 Types of 👣 Crappy Pedestrians

→ The Stop-and-Goers

→ The Angler

The angler constantly walks to the side which forces you to walk at an angle as w to keep from bumping into them.

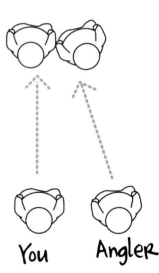

→ The Death Wish

Contrary to popular belief, pedestrians do not always have the right of way.

→ The Pacematching Stranger

Why is he walking at the same speed as me? Christ this is awkward

If this guy doesn't either slow down or speed up I'm gonna kick him in the jewels and then make a run for it.

→ The Text Messenger

They make blind people look like they know where they're going.

→ The Linebackers

Good luck passing them; they walk shoulder-to-shoulder and they're slow as molasses.

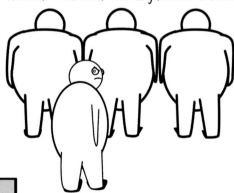

→ The Ogler

How THE MALE ANGLER FISH
gets completely SCREWED

$\mathcal{F}$rom birth, a male angler fish is basically worthless; he's small, weak, and can barely find food.

Hey dood, I'm fresh out of the womb and I generally suck at life. Could you spot me some of that crab you're eating?

I don't even need a decent piece, just let me gnaw on an eye socket or something.

crunch
MUNCH CRUNCH
crunch

$\mathcal{U}$nlike most fish, the male will never grow out of this phase—he'll be hungry his entire life.

Okay, this is such a load of crap. That freakin' sea cucumber over there doesn't even have a brain and it's doing better than I am.

hurrrr

He is born, however, with a great sense of smell, which will be the driving force behind his existence.

What is that damn smell?!!
It's both terrifying and wonderful,
I HATE IT BUT I NEED IT.

The smell is actually the pheromone of a female, which the angler will search for his entire life.

THE SMELL... SO ENCHANTING

GIVES ME FISHRAGE

Behold, the female:

Huge, vicious, and capable,

the female angler can lure in other fish using a glowing spine on top of her head, and then distend her jaws and stomach to devour prey twice her size.

The male, upon seeing her, will realize his calling in life...

My God! She's beautiful!

She's the one!

Finally, my suffering is at an end.

...And he'll start biting her.

I want to kiss you. Or eat you. Maybe a little bit of both.
I don't care, as long as we're together.

Hmm..that's odd. Meh, screw it... I'll just keep biting.

While biting, his lips will start to melt.

Then, his internal organs will also start melting and fuse into the side of the female's body.

OH GOD, WHAT THE SHIT IS THIS?!!

Eventually, his entire body will fuse into hers. The only thing that will remain is a pair of gonads which the female can later use to impregnate herself.

Basically, he becomes a pair of shiny new testicles for the female.

Balls are like snowflakes: They're unique, beautiful, and every animal is only allowed one pair.

The female angler, however, defiles this notion and can fuse with multiple males.

EAH, THAT'S RIGHT. I HAVE NOT ONE, NOT TWO, BUT EIGHT PAIRS OF FISHY BALLS AND I'M HERE TO FUCK SOME SHIT UP.

Meaning she can have as many balls as she wants.

HOW TO SAVE MONEY
$ ~ LIKE A ~ $
CHAMP

Send your kids to a labor camp.

Save money when dining out.

Cut down on heating costs; use your pets to keep warm!

Don't buy expensive prescriptions. Instead, self medicate.

Find a secondary source of income.

FAILED ENTREPRENEUR

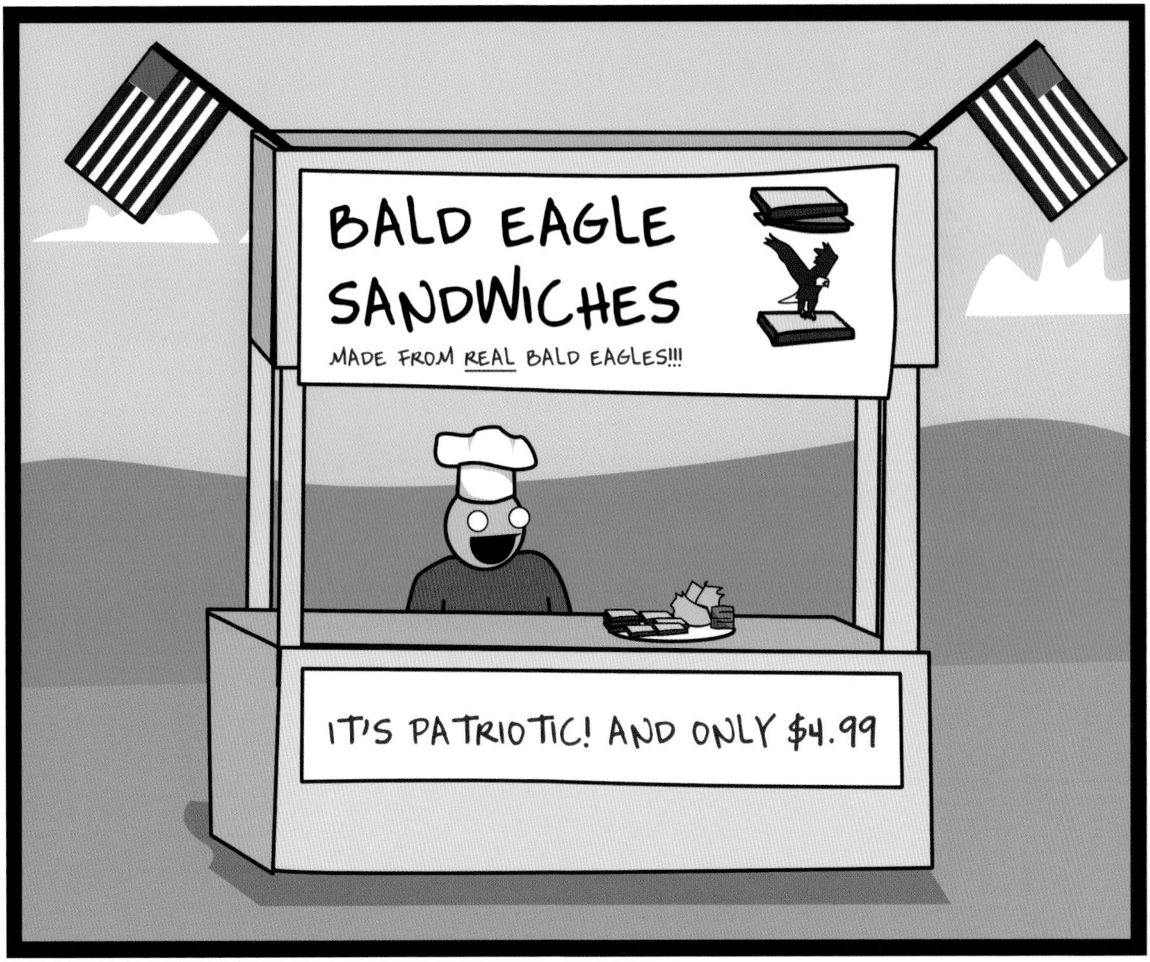
BALD EAGLE
SANDWICHES
MADE FROM REAL BALD EAGLES!!!
IT'S PATRIOTIC! AND ONLY $4.99

5 REASONS TO HAVE
RABIES INSTEAD OF BABIES

YOU CAN'T GIVE BABIES TO YOUR FRIENDS

BUT YOU CAN GIVE THEM RABIES!

BABIES MAKE A FLIGHT UNBEARABLE
BUT RABIES MAKES IT FUN!

BABIES MAKE YOU SLOW

RABIES MAKES YOU FAST!

RABIES STOPS PREDATORS
BABIES DO NOT

YOU CAN'T TAKE A BABY TO THE MOVIES
BUT YOU CAN TAKE RABIES!

REMEMBER FOLKS: **RABIES NOT BABIES**

10 reasons
to avoid talking on the phone

The Courtesies

Etiquette requires you to work through a pile of time-wasters just to ask a simple question.

Hey Bill! It's been awhile. How are you? What have you been up to? How are the kids? HA HA! That's great! Do you still have that magnificent beard? I tried to grow one but my face ends up looking like I dipped my jaw in Vaseline and then gave a raspberry to the underside of a cat. Wow, it's so good to hear your voice...

...20 minutes later

So uh.. the reason I'm calling is - can I borrow your chainsaw?

No.

OK Bill, no problem! Figured it couldn't hurt to ask. Well, it's been great talking to you, and we should meet up for beers sometime. I'd love to gaze upon that enchanting beard over a delicious beverage. We don't talk much anymore, you know? it's a shame. I remember when we used to run and laugh together without a care in the world, like little girls on the first day of summer ...

The Pauses

On the phone, ten seconds of silence feels like ten years of silence.

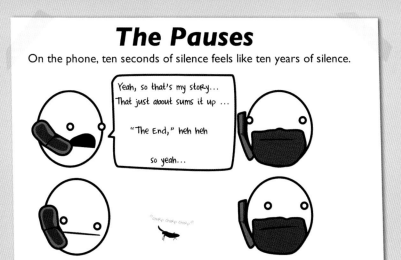

The Jagged

Neither one of you times your responses properly, so you're constantly interrupting one another.

The conversation lacks any kind of flow.

> I really hate it when my wife puts rattlesnakes in the couch. She thinks it's hilarious but their venom is quite powerful and the bites are very painfu-

> -OMG my wife does the same thing, except with scorpions! Sorry, didn't mean to cut you off, sometimes I -

> -Oh no problem! It happe-

> So yeah, "Enough with the goddamn scorpions," I says to her! I thought it woul-

> -I said the same thing! "Honey, rattler bites aren't funny" So what did she do? She swapped out the rattlers for cobras

(complete lack of)
The ↓ Body Language

Body language in conversation can make a huge difference.

VS

The Distracted

There are always those who easily become distracted while on the phone with things like Internet, TV, or other duties.

 What was that noise? Are you at a waterslide park?! I <u>love</u> waterslide parks!

 OH YEAH, it's a waterslide alright. A bad-mexican-food waterslide.

 "Duties," get it? HAHAHA

The Anxious

If you're like me, you can't relax on the phone because you're constantly looking for an opportunity to say goodbye.

...so that's why I don't eat cantaloupe anymore

Neat, Bill. So anyway, I appreciate the call

Hey, you ever try rollerblading in the nude? It pretty much changed my life. Beats the hell out of yoga.

Cool, yeah I'll look into it. Well it's been nice chatting with—

My junk flaps around like a sail. I like to pretend my penis is an eagle, flying free over the mountains of this great nation.

The Lecturer

To some people, the phone is an opportunity to lecture, not to converse.

Usually you can just set the phone down and they won't even notice.

 Blah blah blah raisins blah blah blah lightning storms blah blah blah waffles blarg blah blah blah cat torpedo blah blah blah mango scented candles blah blah blah dragons blah blah blah blah blah blah blah blah blah blah blah....

The Neverending Conversation

Out of politeness, one or both of you will keep a conversation going way past its expiration date.

The Impulsive

You don't have time to think about your responses.

The Epic Goodbye

Just hang up already.

Cool, well thanks for the call.

I'll catch you later

Sounds good dude

You take care of yourself!

Alright bye

Layte!

Peace dude

Like hell you are, we've still got like 20 more ways to say "goodbye"

Adios

au revoir

Yeah man, take care.

We should talk soon

OK, see ya

Will do, catcha later mang

Bye bye!

Goodbye

I'M HANGING UP NOW

Oh ok. Sayounara!

Wiedersehen!

How to Ride a PONY!

Approach Slowly

Do not startle the pony. When up close, gently stroke its head. If you have any dead mice in your pockets, feed them to the pony.

This establishes trust.

Safety First!

If you are carrying a running chainsaw, be sure to flip the kill switch before mounting your pony.

Use Caution

If the pony spits venom in your face or produces a loud roar, it is probably not a pony.

Find another.

How to Mount the Pony

The first time you get on a pony can be tricky, but keep trying and you'll be an expert before you know it!

Do not mount your pony like this. It is wrong.

This is also wrong:
Very, very wrong.

Once on top...

It's OK to fire up your chainsaw. Hold it high and practice your war face.

Be Considerate of Others

If Your Pony Becomes Weary

Mix whiskey with crab blood to create "war juice." Give this to your pony to drink and he'll bounce back in no time.

Ride with Pride

Throughout history our forefathers have always ridden ponies. Remember their triumphs and hold your head high while atop a glorious pony.

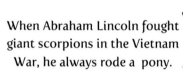

When Abraham Lincoln fought giant scorpions in the Vietnam War, he always rode a pony.

Please take note of his impressive war face.

Just Be Yourself

And don't let anyone tell you what to do.

If they try, show them how handy you are with a chainsaw.

The Final Step

If you've read this far, hold out your right arm and move it over your left shoulder. Once you are able to touch, give yourself a nice pat on the back because...

Congratulations!

You Know How to Ride a Pony!

A pony is the only creature on earth which can shit out a rainbow—and you know how to ride it! Good Job!

How to tell
you're about to get
dumped

New "friends"

This is Chad. We're gonna go play steamrollers in the spare bedroom. Don't come in.

Change in amount of body hair

Hey, why'd you wax your thighs? I like the hair; it helps me exfoliate!

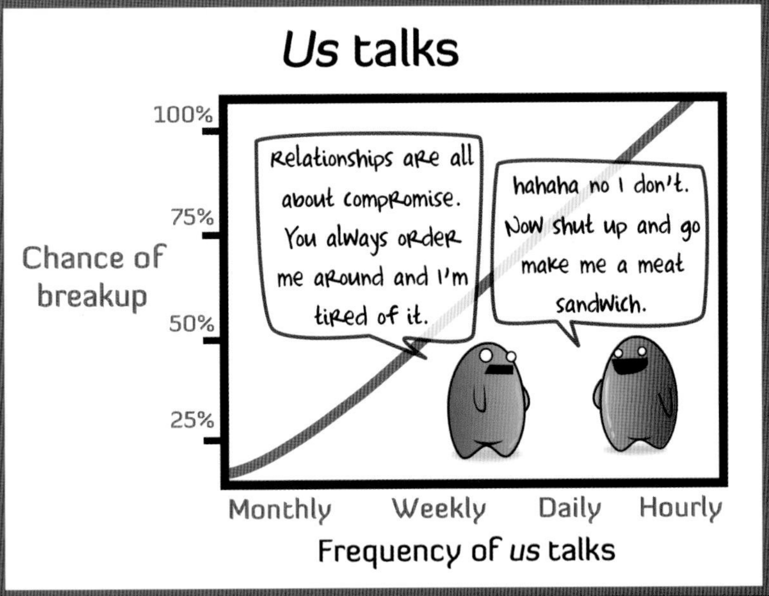
Us talks
100%
75%
50%
25%
Chance of breakup
Relationships are all about compromise. You always order me around and I'm tired of it.
hahaha no I don't. Now shut up and go make me a meat sandwich.
Monthly
Weekly
Daily
Hourly
Frequency of us talks

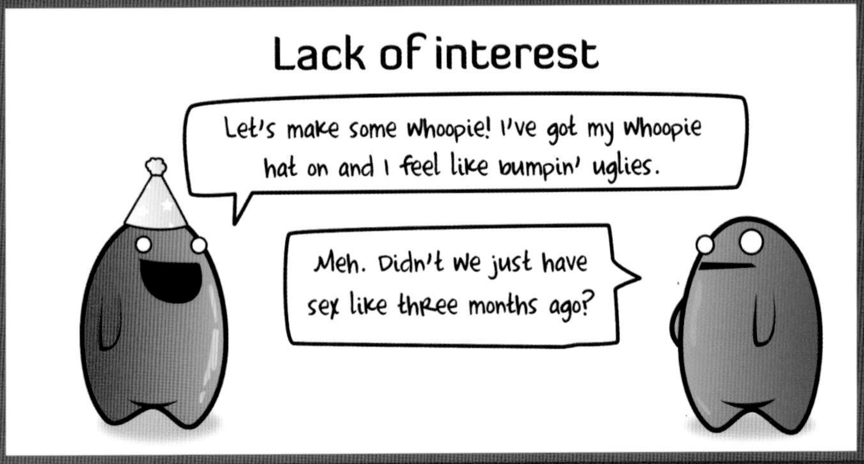
Lack of interest
Let's make some whoopie! I've got my whoopie hat on and I feel like bumpin' uglies.
Meh. Didn't we just have sex like three months ago?

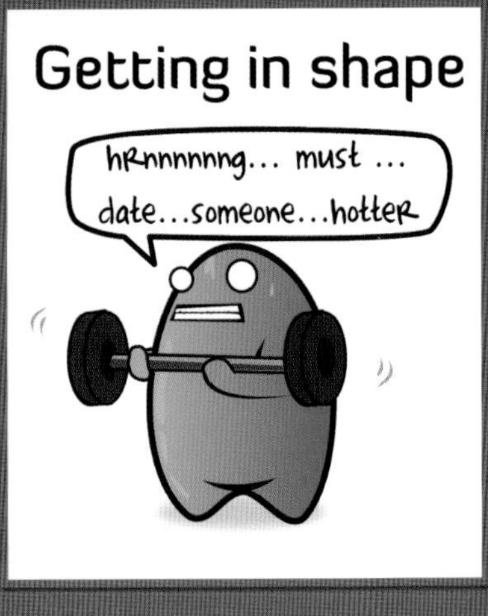
Getting in shape
hRnnnnnng... must ... date...someone...hotter

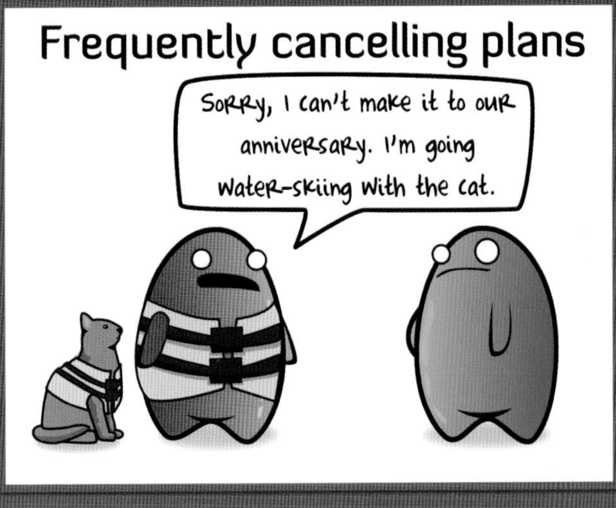
Frequently cancelling plans
Sorry, I can't make it to our anniversary. I'm going water-skiing with the cat.

The 10 types of high fives

(and when to use them)

The Standard Five

Use this when you agree on something trivial, such as how delicious tacos are for breakfast.

The grab-and-shake

Use this when you do something that mutually benefits both of you.

The grab-and-shake with muscle flex

The muscle flex adds an extra level of comradery to the standard grab-and-shake.

Things worked out so well, let's make our biceps wink at each other!

The Fist Bump

Use the fist bump when you want to greet someone but don't want to look like a real estate agent. It adds a degree of hipness to the standard five.

'Sup mang

The Painful Slap

This is useful when you're required to congratulate someone but you secretly resent them.

Hey, you know that Riding lawnmower you've been talking about for months? I bought it! It's AWESOME! It's got 24 gears and even makes protein shakes! HIGH FIVES!

THE TRICK

Use this when you want to get your ass kicked.

The Chest Bump

The chest bump is used when you observe or take part in a victory and agree on the outcome.

The Misfire

This is when your hands don't come together quite right. Use the misfire when you want to look like a complete waste of life.

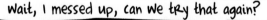

The High Ten

Use the high ten when you've done something *really* impressive.

The Jumping High Ten

ONLY use the jumping high ten when you've done something cosmically amazing.

5 Ways
Mayonnaise
can make your life marvelous

DE-LISH MAYO!

One year on the mayonnaise diet and you'll get to buy all new outfits!

Where's my muu-muu? It's muu-muu time!

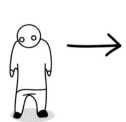

pre-mayo:
super lame!

post-mayo:
super awesome!

Whiter teeth!

KISS ME!

Improved slip and slide

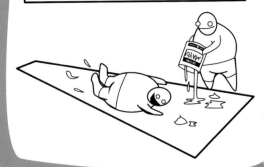

Improved social life

*OH-EM-GEE
He's got a beard made entirely of Mayonnaise! Let's make love to him!*

Shiny, manageable hair!

With mayonnaise, I can make my hair point toward the heavens!

With mayonnaise, I can shape my hair into parallelograms! It really is the best shape

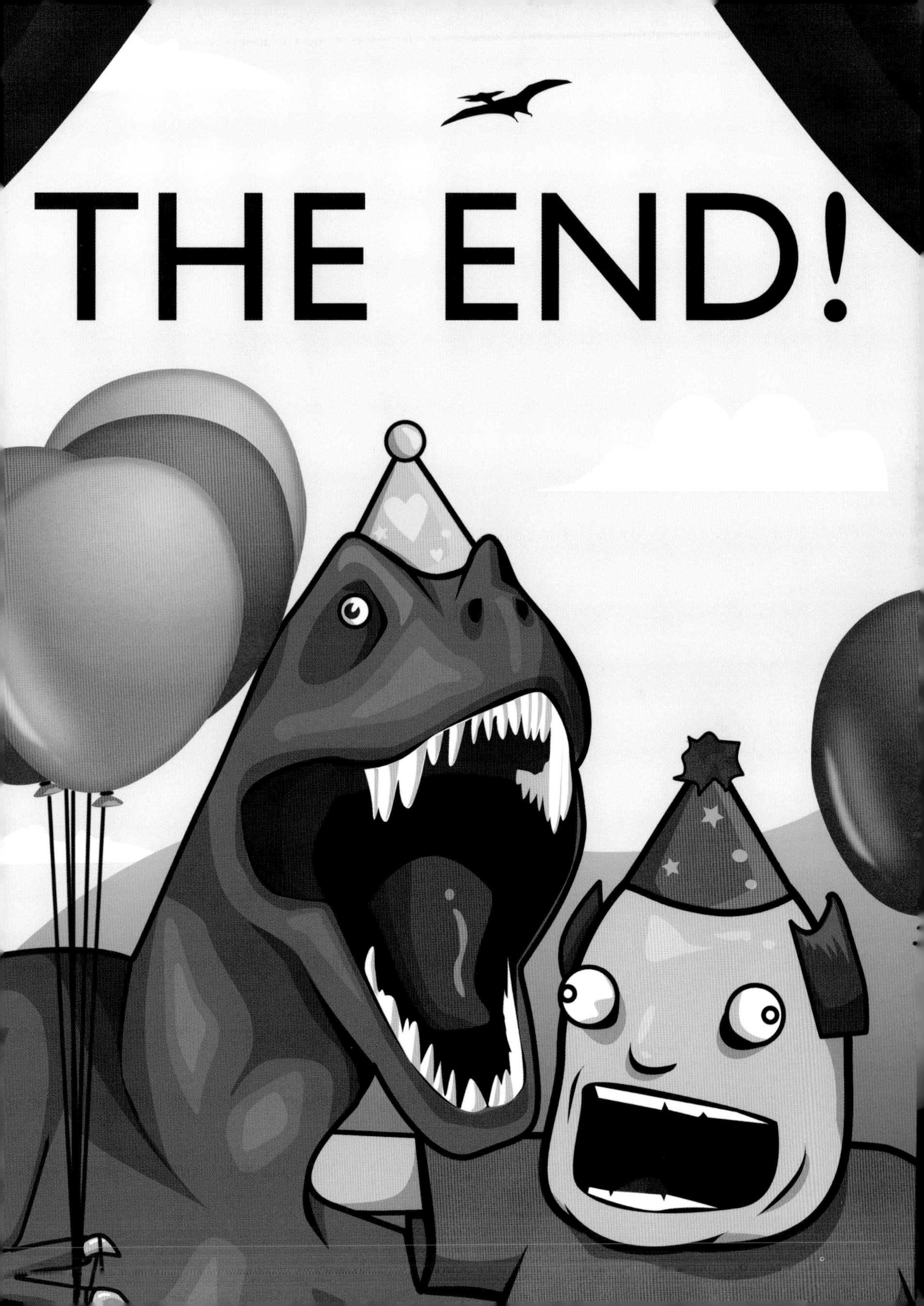
THE END!

The Oatmeal

This book was written and drawn by

Matthew Inman.

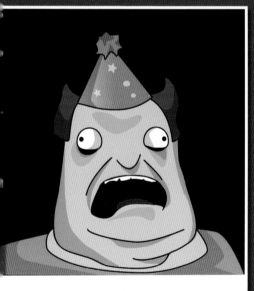

The Oatmeal always wears a party hat, because he's always in the mood to party.

The Oatmeal's real name is Matthew. He lives in Seattle, Washington, and subsists on a diet of dead crickets and whiskey.

He enjoys long walks on the beach, gravity, and breathing heavily through his mouth. His dislikes include scurvy, typhoons, and tapeworm medication.

Visit www.theoatmeal.com for more of Matthew's work.